UNDERSTANDING BIBLE TEACHING
Leadership

G W Kirby MA

Scripture Union

47 Marylebone Lane, London W1 6AX

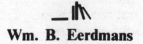

Wm. B. Eerdmans

225 Jefferson Avenue, Grand Rapids, Michigan

ISBN 0 85421 715 0 (Scripture Union)
ISBN 0 8028 1772 6 (Wm. B. Eerdmans)

Printed in Great Britain at the Benham Press
by William Clowes & Sons Limited, Colchester and Beccles

General Introduction

There are many commentaries on the Biblical text and there are many systematic studies of Christian doctrine, but these studies are unique in that they comment on selected passages relating to the major teachings of the Bible. The comments are designed to bring out the doctrinal implications rather than to be a detailed verse by verse exposition, but writers have always attempted to work on the basis of sound exegetical principles. They have also aimed to write with a certain devotional warmth, and to demonstrate the contemporary relevance of the teaching.

These studies were originally designed as a daily Bible reading aid and formed part of Scripture Union's Bible Characters and Doctrines series. They can, of course, still be used in this way but experience has shown that they have a much wider use. They have a continued usefulness as a summary and exposition of Biblical teaching arranged thematically, and will serve as a guide to the major passages relating to a particular doctrine.

Writers have normally based their notes on the RSV text but readers will probably find that most modern versions arc equally suitable. Many, too, have found them to be an excellent basis for group Bible study. Here the questions and themes for further study and discussion will prove particularly useful—although many individuals will also find them stimulating and refreshing.

ONE

Divine and Human Shepherds in the Old Testament

Introduction

In Old Testament times the shepherd was a familiar figure in Palestine. It is not surprising therefore that God is frequently described as the Shepherd of Israel. Good shepherds were renowned for the care and love which they showed towards their flock; protecting them from danger and providing for their sustenance. The term shepherd came to be used of those who were called upon to care for the people of God. Thus Moses was so described (Isa. 63.11). There were those who failed to act as true shepherds to the people, and these are consistently denounced. The faithless shepherd stands under the judgement of God (Jer. 23.1–4; 25.32–38; Ezek. 34).

The same metaphor is carried on to the New Testament where Christ Himself is pictured as the Good Shepherd (John 10).

1: The Shepherd Psalm

Psalm 23

The eastern shepherd occupied a unique position in relation to his flock. Early in the morning he would lead them from their fold to pasture-lands. Throughout the day he would guard them against attacks from wild animals or robbers. At night-fall he would lead them back to the security of the fold. Should one of the lambs be unable to keep pace with the rest of the flock he would pick it up and carry it on his shoulders. Should one of the flock go astray he would search for it until he found it. The sheep and the shepherd were intimately related. The sheep knew their shepherd, and would answer to their names.

In this most familiar of all psalms, David is saying that God is his Shepherd. In saying this he is implying that men need shepherding; that we are, in fact, like sheep all too prone to go astray (Isa. 53.6). The psalmist goes on to say that since the Lord is his Shepherd he will not be in want—his needs will be met.

5

Even in times of danger he will be cared for and protected. An experienced shepherd might take his flock from one pasture to another along a narrow path with perhaps a sheer drop on one side and rugged rocks on the other. So men in life may be constantly surrounded with difficulties and dangers, but with divine companionship they need have no fear.

The eastern shepherd carried a *shebet*, which was club-like in shape, having a large knob on one end. He also carried a staff. With the *shebet* he could defend his sheep against wild beasts, and he might sometimes use his staff to rescue them when they had become entangled in undergrowth, and at other times to give them a gentle tap to ensure that they kept in step with the rest.

This is a person-to-person psalm. It has been said that the heart of religion lies in its personal pronouns. Here are pictured the three great blessings of provision, direction and communion. What more can we need or desire with such a Shepherd as this, a Shepherd who is at one and the same time guide, physician and protector?

Christians can re-echo the psalmist's words with greater emphasis since the Lord Jesus Christ declared Himself to be the 'Good Shepherd' and was prepared to suffer the awful death of the Cross in order to bring us back to God. He has a shepherd's heart of compassion, a shepherd's eye that watches ceaselessly over His flock, and a shepherd's faithfulness that never forsakes or forgets His own. Furthermore, He has a shepherd's strength to lift up those who have fallen.

2: Israel's Plea to her Shepherd

Psalm 80

Opinions vary as to the date of the composition of this psalm. One widely held view is that it was written by a poet from Judah after the deportation of the northern tribes to Assyria, either before or during the Babylonian exile. The 'boar' in v. 13 is probably Assyria. The recurring refrain (3, 7, 19) divides the psalm into three parts.

The first part (1–3) is a prayer addressed to the Shepherd of Israel, seeking the restoration of the divine favour. Jacob had seen God in this role and when speaking to his sons prior to his death he referred to 'the Shepherd, the Rock of Israel' (Gen. 49.24).

In the next section (4–7) the psalmist appears to be in a some-

6

what querulous mood deploring the fact that Israel has become a laughing-stock to her neighbours (6).

In the remaining part of the psalm (8–19) Israel is seen as the chosen vine, which has now become desolate, and the psalmist looks ahead to happier days when that vine will again flourish.

The whole psalm is full of pleas on Israel's behalf, with a wistful looking back to days of prosperity and blessing. The psalmist pleads that the Shepherd will give heed to the bleatings of the sheep and come to their aid.

There is a certain lack of penitence in this psalm. Israel is sorry for herself, but there is little indication that she feels entirely to blame for her sad condition. In days of spiritual and moral declension many of the pleas found in this psalm will find an echo in our hearts, and particularly the recurring refrain.

It is significant that the psalmist makes his appeal to God on the basis of His unique relationship to Israel. This finds an echo in the words of the hymn writer,

> His love in time past forbids me to think
> He will leave me at last in trouble to sink.

Dr. Graham Scroggie aptly entitles this psalm 'Prayer for the recovery of a lost past'. One is reminded of the reference in the prophecy of Joel to 'the years which the swarming locust has eaten' (Joel 2.25).

The reference to 'the man of thy right hand' (17) may well have had a contemporary application, but it finds its fullest expression in the person of Jesus Christ (cf. Heb. 1.13). At meals the master of the feast would place the most honoured guest on his right hand.

If, as has been said, Psa. 80 gives us 'a permanent picture of Israel's woeful condition when banished from God's presence and scattered among the nations', it should also serve as a warning and a rebuke to backsliding Christians whose only plea must likewise be: 'Restore us, O God'.

3: The Lord as the Good Shepherd

Ezekiel 34

It is quite customary in the Old Testament to find rulers described as shepherds, (cf. Isa. 44.28; Jer. 2.8; 10.21; 23.1–6; 25.34–38; Mic. 5.4, 5; Zech. 11.4–17). The very word 'shepherd' suggests both leadership, and caring. Ezekiel has some strong words to say about those shepherds, who, instead of caring for the people had, in fact, exploited them. Such shepherds would receive the divine judgement. They had shown none of the pastoral qualities which were required of them, and instead of keeping the flock together they had allowed them to become scattered. The result was that the people were, in effect, like sheep without a shepherd. Nevertheless, God does still care for His sheep, even though the shepherds appointed by Him have failed. In this passage God is represented as taking on the role of Shepherd to His people. He will seek out the particularly needy sheep—those who have wandered away, and those who are ailing. God is seen here as a God of infinite compassion, tender and loving.

The picture in the latter part of the chapter is of the good shepherd, who will distinguish between the good and bad sheep in His flock. Verses 23 and 24 point to the Messianic Shepherd who gathers the scattered flock together, and leads them into peace and prosperity. This Shepherd was symbolized in earlier times in the person of King David, but he is not merely the historical David resurrected. Christians see in this picture Christ, in His future role as Messianic ruler, ushering in the golden age.

The latter part of the chapter pictures this golden age of unprecedented blessing. It may be compared with similar passages elsewhere (cf. Isa. 11.6–9; Hos. 2.22; Joel 3.18; Amos 9.13ff.; Zech. 8.12). The new era is essentially different, because of a change of shepherd—the blessings envisaged are essentially linked with the coming of the Messiah. Christians usually interpret these blessings spiritually, seeing in them representations of God's gifts to us in Christ. The 'new age' is marked by a 'covenant of peace' (25). This is to be understood in a positive sense pointing to good relationships. God's people will enjoy security under the divine protection. Fears are dispelled. Blessings will abound. The glorious climax to it all is to be seen in the recognition that the covenant between God and the people is once more established (30).

This 'new covenant' is completely unconditional, since it rests solely upon the faithfulness of God. Its provisions are outlined by several of the Old Testament prophets, including Ezekiel (cf. especially Jer. 31.31–34). Within the New Covenant were promises of both earthly and spiritual blessings. In his commentary on the Epistle to the Hebrews, Professor F. F. Bruce remarks: 'The first covenant provided a measure of atonement and remission for sins committed under it, but it was incapable of providing "eternal redemption"; this was a blessing which had to await the inaugu-

8

ration of the New Covenant which embodies God's promise to His people, "I will forgive their iniquity and their sin will I remember no more"' (Jer. **31.**34). The covenant is an everlasting one. Even though its spiritual blessings are already being enjoyed by believers, its complete fulfilment is yet to come.

4: The Rejected Shepherd
Zechariah 11.4–17; 13.7–9

In these passages the spiritual leaders of the people are once more spoken of as shepherds. In ch. 11 Israel and Judah are condemned for their rejection of the Good Shepherd. The message which begins with v. 4 is addressed to Zechariah who is in the line of true shepherds in contrast with the false. The flock of which the prophet is commanded to take charge had been handed over to the slaughterer without a moment's hesitation. Those who had sold the sheep in this way had congratulated themselves on the good prices they had received for them. While Israel is 'the flock doomed to slaughter', even so there is to be found within the nation a faithful remnant ('Grace' v. 7; cf. Rom. **11.**5). From the outset, however, it is clear that the shepherd's effort to save the flock will be a failure.

In the vision Zechariah takes two staves, Grace (lit. Beauty) and Union (lit. Bands). The first staff spoke of the relationship of the flock to their divine Shepherd, while the second symbolized the union of Israel and Judah (cf. Ezek. 37.15–23). The three shepherds (8) may well be three kings, and the mention of 'one month' probably signifies a short space of time. The people are to be left to the fate they have brought upon themselves. God's favour and gracious protection can no longer be assumed. The people as a whole had failed to appreciate the best of shepherds.

Having ceased to serve as a good shepherd the prophet now assumes the role of a worthless shepherd (15), and foresees a reign of terror in the land. As has been pointed out 'if Yahweh is not received as a Shepherd, then another will be, and that other will be a shepherd of doom.'

The immediate fulfilment of vs. 4–14 may have been the period of anarchy which followed on the murder of Pekah, while in vs. 15–17 we may have a reference to the reign of the 'worthless shepherd' Hoshea.

The mention of thirty pieces of silver (12)—the price of an injured slave—reminds us of the price paid at the betrayal of

9

Jesus. He too was rejected by the very people whom He had come to shepherd. One lesson emerges clearly from this otherwise rather difficult passage—Christ cannot be rejected with impunity. As Thomas V. Moore in his commentary on Zechariah observes: 'God may bear long with the wicked, but there is a point where the piling avalanche will cease to be held back, and descend in fearful ruin.'

Some commentators have suggested the two verses (7–9) in ch. 13 might appropriately come at the end of ch. 11. We have here a description of the divine chastisement which is to come upon the people. Whatever the immediate significance of these words may have been, their complete fulfilment is found in Christ. When the Good Shepherd was smitten even His own sheep were scandalized and fled (Matt. 26.31; Mark 14.27; John 16.32). Verse 8 was tragically fulfilled in the destruction of Jerusalem by the Roman army in A.D. 70. We learn from v. 9 that the smaller portion of the people who are saved, are nevertheless called upon to pass through great trials.

Questions and themes for study and discussion on Studies 1–4

1. How did David benefit from being under the Shepherd's tender care?
2. What was the state of the nation when she had strayed from the Shepherd of Israel?
3. Contrast the ways of the shepherds of Israel with the Lord's care for His flock.

TWO

Christ the Pattern of all Ministry

Introduction

A key verse in the New Testament is Mark 10.45 in which our Lord makes clear that He had come 'not to be served, but to serve'. Elsewhere He pointed out that He was among His disciples 'as one who serves' (Luke 22.27). Just before His crucifixion He washed His disciples' feet. In the classic passage of the letter to the Philippians the apostle points out that He took 'the form of a servant'. It is clear that all who profess to follow Him and to serve under Him must of necessity see themselves as servants, since He Himself has set a pattern for all Christian ministry.

5: The Temptation of Jesus
Luke 4.1–21

In this chapter we have a condensed record of the first year of our Lord's ministry. We do not know precisely the amount of time covered by these incidents, but we are given a glimpse of the sort of work He did in the months immediately following His baptism and temptation.

The temptation, while not a part of His public ministry was, nevertheless, part of God's preparation for it. As so often in our experience as Christians, our Lord found that a time of great spiritual blessing may be followed by one of great testing.

There can be no doubt as to the reality of Christ's temptations, even though the manner in which they presented themselves must remain a mystery. Christ found Satan to be very real and in His battle with him He wielded the Sword of the Spirit, which is the Word of God (Eph. 6.17). He referred to God's will as being the all-important consideration, and steadfastly resisted the temptation to depart from, or short-circuit it.

The Devil tempted Him to satisfy His natural appetite by turning stones into bread, but had He yielded to this temptation, there would have been no Gethsemane and no Calvary. Christ was not concerned primarily with His physical needs, but, rather,

11

to fulfil the spiritual purpose for which He had come into the world. The Devil offered Jesus the kingdoms of this world if only He would bow down and worship him, but, here again, the Lord resisted this short-cut to the achievement of the Messianic purpose.

In the third temptation as recorded by Luke, Satan urged Christ to throw Himself down from the pinnacle of the temple. This time the devil himself quoted Scripture, suggesting that He could count on supernatural protection if He would only follow this course. Christ knew that this was no way to draw men to Himself, and, once more, He steadfastly resisted the idea of bypassing God's plan.

The events recorded in vs. 14–22 are only found in Luke's Gospel. They relate to the first visit Jesus paid, after entering on His public ministry, to the synagogue in Nazareth, where He had been brought up. It is noteworthy that His regular custom was to worship in the synagogue every sabbath day. There was special significance in the passage of scripture which He read on this occasion. In voicing the words of Isa. 61 He sought to impress on His Jewish hearers the true character of their Messiah. This prophecy would not find fulfilment in an earthly ruler wielding purely temporal power. He announced that the prophetic passage which He had just read was that day being fulfilled in the presence of His hearers.

No doubt in the synagogue were many of His relatives and friends and it seems that a deep impression was made upon them by the way He spoke. Nevertheless, we do know from other parts of scripture that our Lord was subsequently rejected by His fellow citizens—no prophet is accepted in his own country. Christ's experience in this connection has all too often been repeated in the experience of His disciples.

6: Dealing with Critics
Matthew 12.9–21; 2 Timothy 2.23–26

Much of the opposition which Jesus encountered from religious leaders took the form of 'loaded' questions designed to catch Him out. Often in dealing with these questions He Himself would pose another, the effect of which would show up the absurdity of the original question. One of the points on which the Jewish leaders concentrated was our Lord's attitude to the sabbath.

They appeared to be scandalized when on one occasion He and His disciples went through the cornfields on the sabbath day, and plucked ears of grain because they were hungry. Often those who are bent on opposing the work of God persist in their opposition even though their questions are dealt with. Although Christ clearly answered Jewish criticisms regarding His conduct on the sabbath day, nevertheless, 'the Pharisees went out and took counsel against him, how to destroy him' (Matt. 12.14).

The apostle Paul repeatedly warned Timothy against allowing himself to become involved in 'senseless controversy'. He points out that arguing for arguing's sake serves no useful purpose, but stirs up needless strife. Striving for its own sake has no place in the life of a servant of God (cf. Matt. 12.19). Our aim should always be to win over our opponents rather than antagonize them, and in any Christian leader meekness and patient forbearance should be apparent. In cases where people have been led into error the Christian is concerned to correct them with 'gentleness' in the hope that God may bring them to repentance (2 Tim. 2.25). The Devil has been described as both an intoxicator and captivator of men's minds. He delights to assume the role of an 'angel of light', and in so doing he makes false teaching attractive in the eyes of men. In the final analysis, only God Himself can take the scales from the eyes of those blinded by the Devil in this way, so that they come to see the truth.

The right way to handle opponents should be a matter of concern to all Christian leaders. Paul in giving advice to Timothy foresees that by being kindly disposed rather than aggressive one is more likely to win them over and not antagonize them. It should be the aim of the Christian to be the means, under God, of bringing people to repentance and deliverance from Satan's power.

A Christian worker needs to be able to differentiate between the genuine seeker after truth and the person who loves asking questions and is not over-interested in the answers. Furthermore, he needs to avoid the time-consuming luxury of getting embroiled in controversies which are likely to produce no conclusive solutions.

7: The Servant Role
Mark 10.35–45; Luke 22.24–30

It is significant that when we speak of the work of our Lord here on earth we usually describe it as His earthly 'ministry'. Service

13

was the hallmark of all that He did. He declared 'The Son of Man came not to be served, but to serve, and to give His life as a ransom for many' (Mark 10.45). The word translated 'to serve', the Greek *diakoneo*, literally means 'to wait on tables, to function as a servant'. He told His disciples quite clearly that He was among them as one who served. When in the Upper Room, on the night before His crucifixion, He stooped to wash His disciples' feet, He said to them, 'If I then, your Lord and Teacher, have washed your feet, you also ought to wash one another's feet. For I have given you an example, that you also should do as I have done to you'. (John 13.14f.). He pointed out that while worldly rulers were preoccupied with their status and their authority, this was not to be the case with His followers (Mark 10.42–44). Ministry to Him was literally service.

In the light both of our Lord's example and of His teaching it is somewhat ironical that today the accent is often placed on ministerial status, whereas the pattern of Christian ministry which He so clearly set was one of lowly service. He Himself was happy to take upon Himself 'the form of a servant'. He saw ministry not in terms of status but of function. No doubt He often had in His mind the Servant Songs of Isaiah (42.1–4; 49.1–6; 50.4–7; 52.13–53.12). In them He saw a foreshadowing of His own ministry which was to call for lowly obedience and vicarious suffering. The concept of the servant was never far from His mind, and all the more so towards the end of His earthly life. Because the Lord Jesus Himself was a servant, His disciples should walk in His steps (Matt. 10.24f.). As J. K. S. Reid has pointed out, 'The prototype for the ministry is our Lord Himself; the pattern for all the New Testament has to say about the ministry is what our Lord has to say about His ministry.'

It is significant that in the Christian Church two of the words used to describe those occupying positions of leadership mean servant. Thus, we describe the pastor of a local church as a 'minister' and those who assist him are sometimes given the title 'deacons'. 'Minister' comes from a Latin word meaning servant, and deacon from a Greek word meaning the same.

It is particularly sad when Christian leaders contend for position, as did James and John. As someone has said: 'The greatest prelate in the church is he who is most conformable to the example of Christ, by humility, charity and continual attendance on his flock and who looks on himself as a servant to the children of God' (Quesnel).

8: The Good Shepherd
John 10.1–30

Our Lord had been accusing the Pharisees of spiritual blindness, and He followed up His indictment by relating the parable of the sheepfold and the Good Shepherd. Since the Pharisees had proved to be blind leaders they could also be described as bogus shepherds.

Throughout Scripture the flock is always regarded as ultimately belonging to God, though He may entrust the care of it to others. Down the centuries there have been good and bad shepherds. The sign of a bad shepherd was that he did not care for his sheep, and for that reason was under the divine judgement (Jer. 23.1f.; Ezek. 34.1–6).

Religious leaders have often failed their followers. In every generation we have to be careful to avoid 'the spirit of the hireling' who lacks a sense of responsibility, is cowardly in face of danger, and shows no real concern for his flock. In contrast, the good shepherd knows his sheep, sends them out, shows personal concern for them, and is even prepared to die for them. The sheep, for their part, know him and recognize his voice, and are ready to follow him.

Verse 16 has been the subject of considerable discussion. Two different Greek words are used and in the RSV this fact is rightly recognized by the use of two different English words 'fold' and 'flock'. The sheep 'not of this fold' are presumably non-Jewish believers. Some early Jewish Christians made the mistake of thinking that all believers should be incorporated into the Jewish Christian community and be compelled to submit to Jewish rites and customs (Acts 15). We learn from this verse that the flock of God will be made up of many different groups and certainly not confined to Jewish believers. The Church is truly a multi-racial society.

9: The Lord's Prayer
John 17

We often describe the prayer Christ taught His disciples as 'the Lord's prayer'. In fact, He Himself never prayed it since it was not applicable to Him. He had no sins to confess and, therefore, no need to ask for forgiveness.

The prayer in this chapter could be more accurately described as 'the Lord's prayer', since we know that He Himself prayed it and only He could have done so. In the first five verses Christ is praying for Himself, whilst the remainder of the prayer is for His disciples. The prayer was uttered in the presence of His disciples in the 'upper room' shortly before His crucifixion. There was no sense of failure or defeat on His part as He contemplated His impending death, but rather the note of triumph. He was about to bring to a successful conclusion the work the Father had given Him. Soon He would be leaving this earth, and the responsibility for proclaiming the good news which He was making possible through His death and subsequent resurrection must rest with His followers. This, then, is Christ's prayer for His Church.

It is significant that His first petition is for the Church's holiness. While His disciples must remain in the world they must nevertheless not be contaminated by it. They represent a community distinct from the world. Jesus prayed that God would preserve their essential holiness (15). Christians are called to be 'holy' people in an 'unholy' world (Phil. 2.15).

Christ now turns to the Church's mission, the very reason for its continued existence in the world (18). The Church plays an essential part in God's plan for the salvation of the world. The Church in every generation needs to be reminded of its missionary vocation.

Next our Lord turns to the Church's unity. He longs for the absolute unity of His people. The inherent unity of Father and Son in the Godhead is to be the pattern for the essential unity of believers (22). It must be stressed that this prayer clearly envisages those who are genuine believers (20). It is a unity in the truth. There is a tendency today to look for organizational unity without adequate attention being paid to the biblical basis which true unity demands. Only the Spirit of God can create unity, but Christians have a responsibility to maintain it (Eph. 4.3). Christ's love for us is to be the standard by which we gauge our love for one another.

10: The Strong and the Weak

Romans 15.1–13

Here the apostle is pointing out the responsibilities we as Christians have for one another. There must be mutual concern. Christ

16

is the supreme example of one who did not 'please' or put Himself first (3). Throughout the New Testament there is stress upon living in harmony with one another, and so glorifying God. Note that the word 'please' occurs three times in the opening verses of this chapter. As Bishop Moule has pointed out, this word does not suggest a servile and compromising deference to human opinion, but 'the unselfish and watchful aim to meet half way, if possible, the thought and feeling of a fellow disciple'.

During our Lord's earthly ministry His work was mainly restricted to Jewish people, and in that sense, He was 'a servant to the circumcised' (8). Nevertheless, His purpose was that Jews and Gentiles should unite in praising God, and that Gentiles should join with Jews in acknowledging Him (8–12). In v. 13 Paul uses the title, 'God of hope', and speaks of peace and joy as blessings which belong to the Kingdom of God. Even though Christians may have the clearest intellectual grasp of the gospel it is only through the Holy Spirit that they are enabled to enjoy, in this life, the blessings of the life to come. In this verse we have a picture of the ideal Christian life—being in touch with God, filled with joy and peace and overflowing with hope—a life lived in the power of the Holy Spirit. In so far as Christians keep before them such an ideal they will discover the secret of true spiritual unity and the superficial differences between them will pale into insignificance.

Paul here sets out his 'philosophy' of Christian service. There are many different words and phrases which relate to effective co-operation in Christian work. There were issues then, as there are today, which tend to divide the Lord's people. The apostle makes the point that all who truly believe in Christ, whether Jews or Gentiles, are to receive one another in the Lord regardless of their backgrounds. He calls for mutual tolerance and understanding. Harmony should be the keynote of relationships between Christians, whether strong or weak, Jewish or Gentile. Heathen observers said of the early Christians: 'Behold how these Christians love one another.' When believers are God-centred in their thinking, and truly desirous to do His will and reveal His glory, they will be patient with one another (5f.). We are not, of course, to tolerate evil or blatant error, but we must be ready at times to 'agree to differ' with other Christians on matters of secondary importance, which are open to question— 'In things essential unity, in things doubtful liberty, in all things charity.' How sad it must make the Lord when His children fight 'over matters on which differing opinions may legitimately be held! Real peace is impossible when we are at cross-purposes with fellow Christians.

11: The Divine Condescension

Philippians 2.1–11

This portion contains one of the outstanding Christological passages in the New Testament. It has been suggested that we have here an ancient hymn in rhythmical form (5–11). The context is an appeal for spiritual unity and the demonstration of humility. It is helpful to read the opening verses in a modern rendering. In ancient Greece lowliness of mind was an attitude worthy only of slaves, yet it is an essentially Christian virtue. Those who truly have the mind of Christ are delivered from self-seeking and self-centredness.

The apostle traces the steps which Christ took from the Father's throne to the Cross of shame—seven rugged steps. First, He was in the form of God, or, as we might say, essentially God. He possessed the very essence of Deity from all eternity (cf. John 1.1f.; 8.58; 17.5). Next, He regarded equality with God as something which rightly belonged to Him, and for which He had no need to strive. It is not surprising, therefore, to find Him claiming divine prerogatives, such as power to forgive sins (Mark 2.1–12), or displaying divine attributes such as power over nature (Matt. 8.27).

Then comes the great step of divine condescension. The Greek literally means, He emptied Himself. Various theories have been put forward to explain exactly what this means. One view suggests that He limited Himself to the knowledge and abilities of an ordinary man, but this is clearly not tenable in the light of His miracles and His teaching. Others suggest that He rendered Himself fallible, but, here again, this is not consistent with His claim to be the Truth (John 14.6). It surely means that Christ hid, as it were, for the time being, His intrinsic splendour or, as Weymouth puts it, 'He stripped Himself of His glory'. He took the form of a servant, literally a slave. He exemplified this when He washed His disciples' feet (John 13.1–11). Then, we are told, He was made in the likeness of men, which presumably means that He passed through boyhood and adolescence as other men have done, and had the appearance of a man because He was a true man. But, He condescended yet further—He deliberately chose to die (John

18

10.17–18). Logically He should not have died, since death had come into the world as a result of sin and He was sinless. Furthermore, He chose the most shameful and degrading death the world of that day knew—the death of a common criminal on a Roman gibbet.

So, in these seven steps, we see the love of God in Christ reaching down to the lowest depths for our sakes (2 Cor. 8.9). That is not the end of the story, however, as Paul points out. This same Jesus is exalted to the right hand of God the Father. Nevertheless, the whole thrust of the passage is aimed to emphasize the need for humility; to have the mind of Christ which was summed up by Canon Guy King as a selfless mind, a serving mind, and a sacrificial mind.

12: The Path to Perfection

Hebrews 3.1–6; 5.1–10

Christ the Son is compared with Moses the servant. We are called upon to 'consider Jesus'. Christians are designated here as 'brothers in the family of God, who share a heavenly calling' (NEB). Jesus is described as God's representative among men and men's representative in the presence of God ('apostle and high priest'). In some senses Moses shared a similar ministry, yet his status was far inferior to Christ's. Moses stood in relation to God's household as a servant, whereas Christ held the position of son and heir. Just as the architect of a building is greater than the building he erects, so God the Owner, Master and Builder of the household of which Moses was part, is worthy of more honour than was Moses. Since Jesus is God's Son the same honour belongs to Him as to the Father Himself.

In the second passage the contrast is drawn between the high priests of whom Aaron was an example, and Christ, who is 'a high priest after the order of Melchizedek'. The Jewish high priest was not self-appointed, and in this he was like Christ Himself—divinely appointed to office.

In vs. 1–4, the writer outlines the qualifications for high priesthood, one of which was an ability to sympathize with those whom he represented (2). Professor F. F. Bruce points out that the Greek verb translated 'deal gently' 'denotes in general "the golden mean between indifference and mawkish sentimentality"'. The writer then turns to consider Christ's qualifications for high priesthood. He certainly had to a marked degree the ability to sympathize with His people. In His incarnation He laid aside the dignity and majesty of His Godhead, and for man's sake, as man, He won for us the right of free access to God.

Christ's office as high priest is typified in the king-priest Melchizedek, mentioned first in Gen. 14.18. He met Abraham returning from battle and refreshed him with bread and wine and blessed him. Nothing is said about Melchizedek's ancestry—he appears as a priest in his own right, and not by virtue of physical descent. So our Lord was named by God a high priest after the order of Melchizedek—the Aaronic priesthood had been passed by.

The key verse in this passage is v. 8. The writer has been concerned with the priestly office of Christ and here he tells us what true priesthood involves. His loving obedience to the Father took Him all the way to Calvary. We cannot escape from the fact that obedience may sometimes for us also involve suffering.

13: Patience under Provocation

1 Peter 2.18–25

Peter is instructing Christian slaves to be submissive to their masters, even though they may find themselves cruelly treated at times. They have an example of innocent suffering in Christ Himself, and as His followers they should walk in His steps.

Parts of this passage are reminiscent of Isa. 53. We are reminded of the sufferings of Christ and of how He reacted to them. We are also reminded that He was the sinless One and His sufferings were for our sins.

Commenting on v. 24, Alan Stibbs points out that the statement made here 'confirms the two ideas that the suffering He endured was the penalty due to sin, but that the sins whose penalty He thus bore were not His own but ours. He thus took the place of sinners, and in their stead bore the punishment due to their sin'. In the Old Testament the expression, 'to bear sin', means to be answerable for it, and to endure its penalty.

It is interesting that the expression 'Shepherd and Guardian' is applied to our Lord in v. 25. He is, indeed, the Good Shepherd, who gives His life for the sheep. The word, Guardian, could equally well be translated, Bishop (as AV (KJV)), and, in fact, describes the function of the shepherd, that is, to be an overseer, to show pastoral care for the flock. The Shepherd who died is alive for ever more to take care of the interests of His sheep.

The main thrust of this passage concerns suffering. Christians are called upon not only to suffer, but to do so in the same spirit of patient endurance which Christ Himself displayed. Attention is particularly focused upon Christ's self-control in speech. When we suffer unjustly, it is so often through what we say that we reveal our reactions. Even under extreme provocation our Lord either remained completely silent or spoke with candour and not rancour. None of us can react in this way without the controlling power of the Holy Spirit. We need to learn from Christ that when we are being unfairly or harshly treated, we may remain calm and serene if we commit ourselves, our cause and our persecutors to God.

In v. 25 the contrast between the former condition of Peter's readers and their present condition is clearly portrayed. The straying sheep have been brought back to the true Shepherd, who loves them and watches over them as a faithful guardian.

A Christian who finds himself working for an unreasonable employer and who is ridiculed for his faith may find this passage speaks to him, both by way of warning and encouragement.

Questions and themes for study and discussion on Studies 5-13

1. As Jesus was commencing His public ministry He faced fierce temptations. How far do His temptations reveal the subtlety of Satan?
2. Our Lord came into conflict with the Pharisees over the Sabbath question. What may we learn here about how to deal with similar controversial issues?
3. What is the basic difference between worldly greatness and spiritual greatness?
4. What are the hallmarks of the Good Shepherd?
5. From John 17 pick out seven things which Christ claimed to have done during His earthly ministry.

THREE

The Ministry of the Whole Church

Introduction

The New Testament uses a number of different images to describe the Christian Church. Probably that of 'the Body of Christ' is one of the most significant. As Paul points out, a body 'does not consist of one member, but of many' (1 Cor. 12.14). The overall impression of this illustration is that members of the Christian Church have varied ministries all of which are important. The New Testament does not imply that the Church should be dominated by one personality, but that the ministry should be shared by all the members. Forms of ministry may vary, but all are endowed with spiritual gifts of one kind or another which they are called upon to use to the glory of God under the direction of the Head of the Body, who is Christ Himself.

14: Spiritual Gifts

1 Corinthians 12

Although the subject of spiritual gifts is the main theme in this chapter Paul begins by reminding the Corinthian church that no one can sincerely acknowledge Jesus Christ as Lord unless and until he has been brought to that position by the illumination of the Holy Spirit. All true Christians have, by various roads, been brought to acknowledge Him as such, and this fact in itself gives them a basic unity.

Our spiritual unity in Christ is, however, a unity in diversity, for not all are given the same spiritual gifts. Every Christian, however, is gifted in one way or another, even though there is enormous variety in the gifts. Some are obviously more spectacular than others, and Christians are encouraged to covet the best gifts and not necessarily the most spectacular.

Paul makes clear who the Giver of these spiritual gifts is and why they are given. The bestowal of gifts lies within the sovereignty of God (11). Yet, underlying all the gifts is one basic purpose—

they are to be exercised 'for the common good' (7). In other words, any thought of self-display or exhibitionism is ruled out. There are in the New Testament several different lists of spiritual gifts, none of which is necessarily complete in itself. In this chapter there are, in fact, two such lists. Some Christians who find it difficult to recognize themselves as having any of the gifts mentioned may all too easily have overlooked the word 'helpers' (28). There are in the Christian Church many opportunities for service for those who are prepared to lend a helping hand, but who may never have the limelight.

Paul pictures the various members of the Church in terms of the constituent parts of a human body. All the various parts have a function to perform and belong together, even though their functions are vastly different. Some church members who are less obviously gifted than others may be inclined to develop an inferiority complex, but this is dishonouring to God. Others with some spectacular gifts may tend to adopt the air of superiority, disparaging their fellow members who do not have such spectacular gifts. This is equally dishonouring to God, since each is responsible to accept gratefully the gift he has been given, and to use it to God's glory. Christians within the Body of Christ are interdependent, and not independent.

15: Spiritual Unity

Ephesians 4.1–16

Paul's letter to the Ephesians has more to say than any other about the Church. The apostle speaks of the basic unity which believers have in Christ, enumerating some of the points on which they are essentially one. Because potentially this unity already exists, this does not mean that we may take it for granted. Christians are still human, and have very 'rough edges'. If our God-given unity is to be preserved and enjoyed, we must work at it, and this involves showing lowliness, meekness, patience and loving forbearance (2). Note that the apostle does not call upon his readers to manufacture spiritual unity, but rather to maintain it (3). There is a constant danger, especially in the modern world, that men should sometimes, for reasons of expediency, try to create a spiritual unity which is not of the Spirit's making.

There is a close parallel between vs. 7–12 and a similar list of spiritual gifts in 1 Cor. 12. In neither case does Paul give a complete list, but merely points out that these are gifts of the ascended Lord, and every individual believer is included in the distribution. Furthermore, they are gifts with a purpose—they are given to equip the people of God for effective ministry (12).

Gifts, then, are not an entity in themselves, nor should they become a preoccupation with us. Rather, the ultimate goal of Christian grace is spiritual maturity, described here as 'the measure of the stature of the fullness of Christ.' In other words, a mature Christian is essentially Christlike whatever spiritual gifts he may or may not have. In the process of growing up spiritually we may have our ups and downs and sometimes be tossed to and fro, but as we grow in grace and become more settled in our convictions we should find ourselves more ready to fit in with our fellow Christians within the Body under the Headship of Christ Himself.

Unity is not to be identified with uniformity. Members of the Church are like the members of a human body—they have different functions to perform. In order to fulfil such functions God's people are equipped with a wide variety of spiritual gifts. By the faithful use of these gifts the Church is built up. Christians should grow both in love and unity. In an age when organizational unity tends to be so greatly emphasized, it is salutary to remember that the unity which the New Testament envisages is essentially 'the unity of the faith'. Truth and love are not to be mutually exclusive. We should not neglect truth when we strive for unity.

16: Spiritual Responsibilities
Hebrews 3.12, 13; 10.23–25; 12.12–17

In each of these passages stress is laid upon the responsibility which Christians have for one another. There is always the danger, even in the life of a Christian, of 'falling away from the living God', and, for this reason, we owe it to one another to be mutual encouragers. An isolated Christian is more likely to succumb to the temptation to backslide than one who is regularly in contact with his fellow believers. In a truly Christian fellowship the members have a sincere concern for the spiritual well-being of each one, and will instinctively seek to help one in danger of slipping away.

In the second passage the thought is much the same. Here again, there is the implication that we can waver and lose out

24

spiritually, and we need the kind of provocation which comes from contact with fellow Christians. It is a pity that the word is normally used in an unfavourable sense. The meaning here is that Christians should stimulate one another to be more loving and more involved in good works. The dangers of Christians hiving off and withdrawing from the local fellowship are envisaged here. None of us can ever be a loner, particularly in the light of the days in which we are living. We need the help and encouragement that come from Christian fellowship.

In the third passage the call to be encouragers to those who are discouraged is sounded once more. The exhortation here is couched in Old Testament language without being a direct quotation. As so often in the letter to the Hebrews, the danger of falling away is shown to be very real, and so Christians must be on their guard not only so far as their own lives are concerned, but also on behalf of other members of the fellowship. As Professor F. F. Bruce comments, 'If some incipient sin manifests itself in their midst, it must be eradicated at once; if it is tolerated, this is a sure way of falling short of God's grace, for the whole community will then be contaminated.'

In times of spiritual dearth and moral declension Christians have a special responsibility towards one another. The strong should help the weak. In a materialistic age we need particularly to guard against the folly of Esau who, 'sold his birthright for a single meal'. Christians have a duty to remind one another continually where their priorities lie.

17: Varied Ministries

1 Peter 4.7–11

In this passage Peter is dealing with some of the practical demands of Christian discipleship. Christians are to live in the light of the impending return of Christ. Since time will soon be at an end we should live now in the full enjoyment of God's varied gifts of grace. Love, above everything else, is to be the hallmark of God's children. Christians are consistently called upon to regard love as their top priority, since it is through this that they make their distinct witness to the world (John 13.35). One expression of this love, particularly emphasized in the early Church, was the showing of hospitality to Christians from other places. The implication here is that such hospitality was frequently

25

called for and should be displayed without any sense of resentment.

As in other New Testament passages, it is assumed that Christians enjoy a variety of spiritual gifts by the grace of God. These are to be used to His glory and not to be disregarded. A Christian is a steward of such gifts as are entrusted to him. There is no suggestion here that spiritual gifts are confined to one or two leaders in the local Christian community. The gifts vary considerably—some are to minister through teaching and preaching, while others will be enabled to serve the Lord through acts of practical kindness. Those who speak must do so with a due sense of the solemnity of the occasion, since they speak in God's name. Those who exercise a ministry along practical lines should be ready to recognize the divine source of the abilities which they have been given. Whatever form our Christian service may take, the aim and object of it should be the glory of God.

In this passage the most significant phrase is 'good stewards of God's varied grace'. This underlines the fact that all the endowments we may have we hold in trust, and, furthermore, it shows that our forms of ministry may vary considerably. It is a great mistake to imagine that we are all called to the same kind of service. We should neither envy nor despise those who have gifts that differ from our own. As Paul points out elsewhere, God in any case is sovereign in the bestowal of such gifts (1 Cor. 12.11).

Probably one of the hardest lessons to learn is how to respect individuality and at the same time preserve unity. The plan of God for His people is that they should enjoy 'diversity in unity'. We must avoid the temptation of trying to cast everyone in the same mould.

Questions and themes for study and discussion on Studies 14-17

1. How would you describe a spiritual gift? (1 Cor. 12).
2. Point out some of the defects in character which militate against the enjoyment of spiritual unity (Eph. 4).
3. What should our attitude be towards those facing special trials? (Heb. 12.12–17).

FOUR

Paul's Principles of Ministry

Introduction

In 2 Corinthians we see how intimate a relationship existed between Paul the pastor and his people, the church at Corinth. Although Paul had a lowly estimate of himself (Eph. 3.8), he never belittled the ministry with which he had been entrusted, and never shrank from those aspects of it which caused him pain. He could never have been accused of seeking cheap popularity, because he realized that stewards must always be faithful and sometimes this involves administering a rebuke.

18: A Ministry of Suffering

2 Corinthians 1.1-11

The church at Corinth consisted mainly of Gentiles with little or no education—they found it difficult to keep true unity, and also to maintain a high moral tone against the background of a corrupt society. In Greek plays a Corinthian was usually pictured either as a drunkard or a prostitute. It is not surprising that Paul's converts at Corinth were a special concern to him. The church was founded during the apostle's stay of eighteen months (Acts 18.1-11). Some five or six years later it seems Paul paid a further visit, but, in the meantime, he was in correspondence with the church. It is likely that Paul wrote more than the two letters we have, including a 'painful' and severe letter which we do not possess. As he writes in this second letter the apostle is contemplating a further visit to Corinth and the letter seeks to prepare the way. In the meantime he has had a report from Titus and has been somewhat encouraged by it.

After the customary greetings and thanksgiving Paul immediately turns to the subject of suffering and testifies to the grace of God which has sustained him at times when he has been afflicted. He points out that suffering equips us for a ministry to others. The Christian is called upon to endure the same kind of suffering

27

as Christ endured (cf. Matt. 20.23)—although, of course, without atoning significance—but the divine comfort is always sufficient for the occasion. Speaking of his own suffering Paul says, 'we were completely overwhelmed, the burden was more than we could bear, in fact, we told ourselves that this was the end' (v. 8, J. B. Phillips). We do not know exactly the form that this suffering took, but probably the people to whom he was writing were familiar with it. It is clear that Paul had faced some extreme danger, which almost cost him his life, and which partially unnerved him—it was such that only God could deliver him, and He had done so in answer to the prayers of the Christians at Corinth. Because of what God had done for him the apostle was encouraged to believe He would continue to help him.

It is noteworthy how grateful he was for the intercession of his Christian friends. Prayer is one of the most effective means we have at our disposal for encouraging others. Christians should particularly pray for their leaders and for those involved in the thick of the battle. Christian leaders in turn should recognize how much they depend on the love, loyalty and prayerful support of their followers. Paul makes it clear that he needed the prayers of the Corinthian Christians.

19: A Faithful Minister

2 Corinthians 1.12–2.17

Paul is defending his integrity. He points out that his ministry has not been prompted by self-interest; he has not been motivated by selfish considerations; he was not a man to go back on his word; he was not one to say yes and no in the same breath any more than Jesus Christ was a 'yes' and 'no' person. Christ did not waver in His purpose, and neither should His servants.

Paul makes it clear that the purpose of his ministry is not to domineer, nor to cause unnecessary pain. He comes to his followers not as a dictator, but to be helpful and bring encouragement. Nevertheless, there must be discipline in the church. It is not stated specifically what the offence was which was then causing tension in Corinth, but there was clearly a church member who had caused the apostle grief. While Paul bore him no malice, he made it clear that he was unwilling to pay a further visit to the church until the problem had been settled. He recalled the tensions he had faced on a previous visit and he did not want a repetition of this. Since that visit he had written a letter to the offender, and possibly to the whole church, regarding his conduct, and all he sought was genuine repentance on the part of the offender. It was not only Paul who had been upset by this man's actions; the whole church had been affected (cf. 2 Cor. 2.5). If the man were to be forgiven, then the church as a whole would have to receive him back into fellowship, and Paul urges the Corinthians to do this, lest he be 'overwhelmed by despair' (7). He should be brought back again to the Christian community and encouraged in Christian service. Paul urges them to reaffirm their love for him (8). Since God has so freely forgiven us, we must be ready to forgive others. If we fail to do so, we give Satan an advantage in the church.

In the closing verses of this chapter Paul strikes a different note. He expresses his jubilation as being comparable to the triumph of a Roman general. When a conqueror returned from battle he was often given the privilege of marching his victorious troops through the city of Rome. Special sacrifices were offered in his honour and the air was heavy with the odour of incense. To the victorious soldiers the incense was an odour of life for they were sharing in the spoils of victory. To the unfortunate victims chained to the wheels of the chariots the incense was the odour of death, for they would be facing execution. Paul and his colleagues were 'a sweet savour of Christ' (15), but to those who refuse the gospel they were a savour of death. Paul ends this passage by underlining the sincerity of his ministry. He spoke from his heart, and did not seek to make capital out of his preaching. He spoke as from God and in his ministry there was no trace of professionalism.

20: A Minister of the New Covenant
2 Corinthians 3

In this passage the apostle raises the question of testimonials. He is not particularly interested in references as such. His converts were themselves a testimony to the genuineness of his missionary activity. The only Bible the world reads is written on the lives of Christian people. Paul's confidence was not in himself—he was but the instrument which God had used. By the grace of God alone he was what he was.

Paul saw himself as a minister of the New Covenant inaugurated by Christ on Calvary. This was essentially a spiritual covenant to be proclaimed by men who had been quickened by the

29

Spirit. The letter of the Old Covenant served to condemn men, while the Spirit under the New Covenant communicates life. Herein lies the essential difference between the law and the gospel. Although the law given through Moses condemned, it had a necessary function in the education of man's moral sense. Furthermore, it reflected the character and purpose of God. The greater glory of the New Covenant, however, lay in its superior function. Under the Old Covenant man was convicted of sin, and was condemned; under the New he is made right with God. The difference is between condemnation and righteousness. The splendour of the Old Covenant is eclipsed by the glory of the New, so much so that by comparison the Old hardly appears glorious at all (10). Because he is living under the New Covenant Paul is confident, courageous and outspoken. Moses had to veil his face to hide the fading glory but now it is different. Whenever a Jew turns to the Lord and sees in Him the perfect fulfilment of the Mosaic Law, the veil is removed. Paul goes on to speak of the transformation taking place daily in the lives of those who are indwelt by the Holy Spirit. This transformation comes about when the believer contemplates the glory of God in the face of Jesus Christ, and is essentially a spiritual transformation. The Christian life is progressive in that the disciple becomes more and more like his Master. There is a sense in which we are already saved; another sense in which we are being saved, and yet another sense in which we are yet to be fully saved.

In v. 6 Paul has condensed into a brief sentence New Testament teaching about the law and the gospel. He expounds this more fully in Rom. 7 and 8. It is tragic when Christians, who should be living in the light of the New Covenant and the freedom which it brings, lapse into legalism. As one commentator has put it, 'When the sun has risen, the lamps cease to be of use'. This is an overstatement but the point is clearly made. As Christians we have not been brought into bondage to a new set of laws, but through a changed heart we have been made into new men.

21: A Christ-centred Ministry
2 Corinthians 4

The fact of having been entrusted with the task of proclaiming the gospel precludes faintheartedness. Such a ministry is an undeserved and gracious gift of God. There is no room for 'disgraceful underhanded ways' (2). Paul's methods were always open and above-board—he did not act like the double-dealing politician or unscrupulous salesman. He did not dilute the Word of God in order to be popular, but presented the truth directly and faithfully.

A preacher's task is to draw attention not to himself, but to Christ—the only one who has a right to the believer's total allegiance. Paul was a preacher because of what God had done for him through Christ, and he longed to pass this on to others.

There is a contrast between the message and the messenger. The treasure of the gospel has been entrusted to men subject to human frailty (7). Paul speaks of the circumstances in which he often finds himself, but testifies to the strength given to him to meet such situations. He may be 'hemmed in on every side' but is not immobilized. Paul took his life in his hands—but a supernatural power, the very life of Jesus, was being manifested in him. His sufferings were a source of life to those to whom he ministered. Paul simply could not abandon the ministry of the Word. Everyone who himself has faith has a witness to bear to God (cf. Psa. 116.10).

For the apostle even the prospect of death held no terrors. His real objective was the eternal welfare of his converts. He does not 'lose heart' although his sufferings are exhausting—his body may show signs of wear, but his inner nature is constantly renewed. In the light of heaven's glory, passing afflictions pale into insignificance. The afflictions are transient, but his inheritance in heaven is unfading.

We cannot but marvel at the lowly estimate Paul had of himself —'a common, clay pot'—but he also knew he was 'a chosen vessel' (Acts 9.15), and he never belittled the ministry with which he had been entrusted. He never ceased to wonder at God's grace in saving him and commissioning him. It is still true that God's saving truth is entrusted to very ordinary people—people like ourselves; common 'earthenware jars', as it were.

It is a battle in which we are engaged. Yet there is no reason to lose heart. As J. B. Phillips has rendered it, we may be 'knocked down but not knocked out'. The Christian refuses to give way to despair. Christ's words about the corn of wheat falling into the ground and dying (John 12.24) are applicable to Christian service, but the follower of Christ is concerned with that fruitfulness which will bring glory to God.

22: A Ministry of Reconciliation

2 Corinthians 5

Paul is conscious of his failing faculties and the imminence of death—our human bodies are only temporary structures; they are as vulnerable to wear and tear and decay as a tent. The apostle looks forward to his eternal shelter—his resurrection body. He thinks of his spiritual body as a garment to be put on, and longs for the more permanent dwelling which will be his after death.

Paul's intense desire is to enjoy the protection of an imperishable heavenly shelter, but this does not mean he has a fanatical desire to be rid of his present human body. For the time being he is in this tent, but he desires to be better clothed to enjoy the fuller life of heaven.

He speaks of the Holy Spirit as being the 'guarantee' of future blessing. We are, therefore, to be 'of good courage' because of the Holy Spirit's indwelling presence. While the Christian is already 'in Christ' he is not yet 'with Christ'. Nevertheless, our aim, come life, come death, should always be to please our Lord (9). We must all appear before the *bema*—the judgement seat of Christ.

Paul was deeply conscious of his accountability to Christ. He was fearful of letting Him down, of being a disappointment in the eyes of the One who had done so much for him. As Christians we are not in danger of the judgement of the 'great white throne', which results in condemnation, but our faithfulness in service will be under review. The quality of the work we do for Christ is even more important than the quantity.

Paul had in Corinth those who were only too ready to denigrate him. His followers could, however, contrast his real devotion and integrity with the supposed superiority of these rival teachers. Paul was constantly under the all-compelling constraint of Christ's love for him. As a Christian he no longer views men and women solely in the light of appearances. He knows that a true believer is in fact a new creation, fundamentally different from what he once was.

A preacher of the gospel may be properly described as an ambassador for Christ. 'An ambassador is at once a messenger and a representative. He does not speak in his own name. He does not act on his own authority. What he communicates is not his own opinions or demands, but simply what he had been told or commanded to say. But at the same time, he speaks with authority, in this case the authority of Christ Himself' (Hodge). God makes His appeal to men through men. Necessary qualities in those who are ambassadors for Christ are tact, dignity, and courtesy. There must be no bludgeoning or bullying.

In this fifth chapter Paul gives us two statements which sum up the message of the gospel—'God was in Christ, reconciling the world to himself' and 'If any man is in Christ, he is a new creation'. Inevitably we are brought face to face with Christ's death, for here is the basis which makes reconciliation possible. Not only do we see the love of God revealed in a unique manner, but we find here the means whereby the law of God has been satisfied. Where this good news is believed and acted upon lives are transformed. The most dramatic and radical change is in the very motivation of life. The 'natural' man's life revolves round himself; he is motivated by self-interest, whereas the Christian's life revolves round Christ, and he lives to please Him. How desperately in the modern world we need to show men and women this new way which not only brings them into a right relationship with God, but also with one another!

23: A Responsible Ministry

2 Corinthians 6.1–10

In this passage we see the marks of a faithful ministry. Paul has already reminded the Corinthian church of his call to be an ambassador for Christ (5.20). As such, he, and the apostles generally, are God's fellow-workers. He appeals to the Corinthians not to let the Christian message pass them by, and he underlines the urgency of his appeal by quoting from Isa. 49.8—the accepted time will not always be with us.

He goes on to stress the importance of ministers not giving unnecessary offence or bringing the ministry into disrepute—'There are people who will be glad of an excuse not to listen to the Gospel, or not to take it seriously, and they will look for such an excuse in the conduct of its ministers' (Denney). The characteristic virtue of the ministerial office should be steadfast endurance, even in the face of afflictions, hardships and frustrations. Some trials are of a general nature, but some are inflicted by others, whilst there are also trials that are self-inflicted in the cause of the gospel.

Paul goes on to refer to the spiritual graces which God enabled him to display as a minister of Christ. These included singleness

33

of purpose and patience with people. Sometimes the apostle's reputation stood high, but at other times the opposite was true. He knew what it was both to be defamed and to be betrayed; to be treated as an impostor, and yet true; ignored by some, yet well-known to others; brought face to face with death, yet very much alive; a man to be pitied in the eyes of men generally, yet full of joy; although he was poor so far as this world's goods are concerned, yet he possessed the unsearchable riches of Christ.

In these verses Paul gives us a series of vivid contrasts between the Christian and the man of the world. In the eyes of the world the Christian is to be pitied, and yet the man of the world has no conception of the joy of the believer. A keyword here is endurance (*hupomone*). It is a difficult word to translate, but as William Barclay comments: 'It describes the ability to bear things in such a triumphant way that it transfigures them and transmutes them.'

24: A Holy Ministry
2 Corinthians 6.11–7.3

In this passage Paul is appealing for consistency of life and true consecration to the Lord. It is essentially a personal appeal. He points out that he has spoken to them without reserve. His heart goes out to them and he asks that in return they shall feel the same affection for him.

He has some clear-cut advice regarding associations with un-believers. There must be no permanent relationship formed because believer and unbeliever do not have a common basis in life. He is probably thinking primarily of mixed marriages, but some have applied the same teaching to business partners. Obviously there must be social contact between Christians and the non-Christian world, but as one translator has it, we should 'stop forming intimate and inconsistent relations with un-believers'.

It is interesting to note that in this passage four different words are used to show why such a relationship is 'unequal'. The words used embody two ideas—harmony and sharing. On both these counts a close union between Christians and non-Christians is ruled out. As regards marriage, Paul's counsel is clearly addressed to those, who, as yet, have not entered a marriage contract, because elsewhere he makes it clear that Christians must uphold a relationship which already exists, unless the unbelieving partner wishes to terminate it (1 Cor. 7.12f.).

The call to Christians is to separate themselves from evil and turn fully to God. The word 'defilement' (7.1) is widely inclusive and covers, not only the outward things that all are able to see, but also the inner motivation.

Separation is not a popular doctrine among Christians today, partly because it has sometimes been construed too narrowly. Nevertheless, as Denney has said, 'There is no conception of holiness into which the idea of separation does not enter'. If we are, in fact, to be separate to God, it means by implication that we are to be separate from sin and, in some degree, from sinners. The apostle is pleading for consistency on the part of believers and also for integrity. If we are going to enjoy an intimate family relationship with God, we must recognize its implications, and, therefore, be separate from all that would grieve our Heavenly Father.

In the concluding verses of this passage Paul makes a series of claims—he has wronged no one, corrupted no one, taken advantage of no one. His hands are clean. He tells the Corinthians how full of joy he is even though he is assailed by troubles on every side. There is great comfort in knowing we have not been the means of causing others to stumble but rather have pointed them in the right direction.

25: A Ministry of Correction

2 Corinthians 7.4–16

Paul has been comforted by the news he has received from Titus of the church in Corinth. We see him here as a very sensitive minister of the gospel, who feels deeply for his people. He rejoices that they have turned back to God. Earlier, he had occasion to send them a letter, the full contents of which we are ignorant of, but which clearly had some very straight things to say to the church. He had not enjoyed writing such a letter, but he rejoices now to know that it had had the desired effect, causing much sorrow when it was read, but at the same time urging them to repentance.

Paul is an example to us of moral courage in that, although he was himself a sensitive person, he did not flinch from expressing himself strongly when occasion demanded. He could never be accused of being a man-pleaser. In this respect, he is a shining example to all who are called to the pastoral office.

In the passage before us, he draws a distinction between mere human remorse and godly grief, which alone produces true repentance. He points out a number of ways in which the Corinthians demonstrated the genuineness of their repentance. They had taken sin seriously and had redressed the wrong in the church. They had also displayed a new and revived interest in spiritual things, which had replaced their indifference and apathy.

We have a pointer here to the matter of church discipline, which is often sadly lacking today. Such discipline is not to be exercised merely in the interest of the offending member, but for the good of the church as a whole. In this section we find a summing-up of the whole unhappy affair, which had caused strained relationships between Paul and the church. Confidence has now been restored. If we are eager to see greater discipline exercised in the Christian Church today may we be equally concerned that it should be administered by those who have as sensitive a spirit as the apostle.

Paul speaks of his pride in the church and we can understand what he means. His confidence has been restored and the same man who administered rebuke is now sounding forth the praise of the church. No doubt we can all think of churches that cause pain to those who minister to them, but there is a place for pride in a church fellowship, not the pride of self-glory, but the justifiable pride which acknowledges a work of grace coming to fruition in the hearts and lives of the people of God.

Questions and themes for study and discussion on Studies 18-25

1. What should be the motives of a pastor when he feels called upon to rebuke his people?
2. What is conveyed by the expression 'ambassadors for Christ'?
3. What is the apostle's attitude towards growing old?
4. How should the fact of personal accountability to God affect our lives?
5. What does Paul teach about separation from the world?

FIVE

The Ministry of the Apostles

Introduction

Clearly the apostles occupied a unique position in regard to the establishment of the Christian Church. Numbered among them was Saul of Tarsus, who described himself as 'the least of the apostles, unfit to be called an apostle' (1 Cor. 15.9), yet, nevertheless, one who was surely the greatest missionary the world has ever known.

26: The Mission of the Twelve

Matthew 10

The chapter opens with the charge given by our Lord to the twelve apostles. Matthew lists them in pairs, possibly corresponding to the groups into which they were formed when Jesus sent them out two by two (Mark 6.7). Thaddaeus or Lebbaeus probably corresponds to the Judas mentioned by Luke (Luke 6.16). Judas may have been his original name, which was later changed because of the stigma attached to the other Judas. Basically, the apostles were charged to go out with no reserve comforts, no second staff, no second pair of shoes, no change of clothing. When they entered into a town they were told to stay in one particular home, probably to prevent different people trying, with ulterior motives, to have a share in entertaining them. They were to use the usual Semitic greeting, 'Peace be unto you.' In cases where they were not received they were to shake the dust from their feet, no doubt as an indication that they had been staying on what was virtually heathen soil.

In their behaviour they were to be both wise and guileless. They could expect a measure of persecution, but they could depend upon words being given to them when they would be hauled before magistrates. The prospect before them was frightening in one sense, but in facing persecution and trials they were simply walking in the steps of their Master. They need not be afraid, for God's loving care would surround them and, in due time, they would have their reward. Furthermore, those who showed hospitality to them, even in the smallest degree, would be rewarded as though such hospitality had been shown to Christ Himself.

One thing that emerges from this passage is the divisive result of Christian discipleship, particularly in family relationships. There is a sense in which Christ unites, and another sense in which He divides. Even those of different races find unity in Christ, whereas members of the same family may be divided because of Him.

Disciples cannot expect to fare better than their Master. Those who go out in His name will not always find a ready acceptance, either for themselves or their message. They must be prepared to risk losing the favour of men and even face the possibility of losing life itself in the cause of Christ. The day will come however when the tables are turned, and those prepared now to confess Christ will be confessed by Him before the Father, while those who now deny Christ will similarly be denied.

The object of Christ's first coming was not to set up a millennial kingdom, but to proclaim a message which would often lead to strife and division. We must not blame the gospel for this, but the heart of fallen man. Christians cannot escape cross-bearing— to follow Christ one must be willing to deny oneself.

27: Apostolic Prerogatives

Matthew 16.13–20; John 20.19–23

Unlike the Scribes and Pharisees who had 'taken away the key of knowledge' and 'shut up the kingdom of heaven against men' (Luke 11.52; Matt. 23.13) Peter was to use the keys to open it, and he did so first to the Jews (Acts 2.38ff.), secondly to the Samaritans (Acts 8.14ff.), and then to the Gentiles (Acts 10, 11; cf. 15.7). The Reformers rightly maintained that this authority given to Simon Peter was in fact through him passed on to the Church, and was virtually a commission to proclaim the Word of God. Similarly the function of binding and loosing is not the function of an order within the Church, but of the gathered company of believers. What is essential to the validity of any binding or loosing is not the official status of those who do it but the presence and authority of Christ among them.

Some would argue that, while this prerogative was not given to Peter exclusively, it was a commission given to the apostles as a whole and confined to them.

Whether we hold to the view that this is a continuing commission given to the Church as a whole, and relating to the exercise of discipline, or was confined to the original apostles, we cannot on any count accept the suggestion that Christ had in mind here the perpetuation of a priestly caste endowed with special rights by virtue of the office held.

When it comes to the forgiving and retaining of sins (John 20.22f.) Christ's commission here clearly was one to the Church as a whole rather than to a limited group within it. It is the function of the Church as a corporate body to declare forgiveness to those who truly repent; even though the declaration may be made through the voice of certain individuals. There is no evidence in the New Testament that the apostles believed unique authority had been given to them in this connection. They could and did, however, declare authoritatively the terms on which God would forgive men's sins. It is God who forgives men through Christ; it is the Church which proclaims His forgiveness.

It is clear that the proclamation of forgiveness of sins through Christ was to be a leading feature of the apostolic commission, as it had been in our Lord's own ministry.

The giving of a key to a scribe was symbolic of bestowing authority to teach. To bind meant to make a precept an obligatory law, while to loose was tantamount to declaring a precept not binding.

As those who had received the benediction of Christ's peace and been promised the gift of the Holy Spirit, the disciples could now truly become apostles and, like their Master, exercise a ministry of reconciliation.

28: Catching Fish and Feeding Sheep

John 21

Some commentators speak of this chapter as an epilogue to the Gospel since the last verse of the previous chapter appears to conclude the narrative. The disciples, in obedience to Christ's instructions (Mark 16.7), had returned north to Galilee, but He had not yet appeared to them. Peter, restless, perplexed and nervy, says, 'I am going fishing.' It was a natural enough reaction on the part of a man whose livelihood had been in the fishing industry. There was little that you could teach Peter about the fisherman's art. Strangely enough, however, a night's fishing proved singularly unfruitful—he and his companions caught precisely nothing. Now, with the same men using the same boats success dramatically followed on failure. The Lord Himself had intervened and they had been obedient to His command. The precise figure of fish caught suggests a symbolical significance, but none of the various interpretations put forward is very convincing.

Later in the chapter we read of how the disciples accepted the Lord's invitation to have breakfast, and some have read into this account a eucharistic emphasis. After that Peter was asked three times by Jesus whether he really loved Him. Different Greek words are used and opinions are divided as to whether there is any real difference in meaning. In the first question Simon is asked whether he loves Jesus, (*agapao*) and replies by saying that he feels a real affection for Him (*phileo*), and, again, this is repeated the second time. The third time Jesus uses the same verb, asking Peter whether he has an affection for Him and receiving the assurance that this is so. Our Lord is saying, in effect, 'Are you quite sure that you have an affection for me?' This question is the preliminary to a commission to serve. Before we can enter the service of Jesus Christ we need to be sure of our motivation. Too much Christian service is done from a sense of duty, and even sometimes with a spirit of drudgery, whereas the true motivation for serving the Lord should be the constraint of divine love.

It is interesting that in this chapter we should find a reference both to catching fish and later to feeding sheep. These two metaphors are both applied in the New Testament to Christian service. When Peter and Andrew were originally called by the Lord He told them He would make them 'fishers of men' (Matt. 4.19). Now, Peter is commissioned to feed Christ's sheep, which is the privilege and responsibility of every true pastor.

Having commissioned Peter, our Lord reminded him of the costliness of discipleship. Very literally he will walk one day in his Master's steps. He is given a clear indication that he will suffer martyrdom. John Marsh comments: 'To be a disciple is not just "following Jesus"; it is to be his "fisherman", to share in his own gathering of the messianic community; it is to suffer with the

Messiah in the all-decisive messianic woes; it is to witness by life and by death, to the victory of the crucified.' One cannot but feel that we have rather lost this note and tended to glamorize the ministry, emphasizing the 'glory' of it rather than the 'suffering servant' aspect.

29: Put in Trust with the Gospel

Ephesians 3.1–13

Paul's theme here is the divine mystery which has now been revealed, and which he himself had received by special revelation. This mystery consisted in the fact that in the Christian Church there is to be a welcome on equal footing for Jew and Gentile alike. This 'Good News' Paul sees as a sacred deposit with which he has been entrusted. He never ceased to marvel that, by God's grace, he, of all people, had been commissioned to preach and to declare, to the Gentiles in particular, 'the unsearchable riches of Christ'.

In v. 8 we learn what Paul thought about himself. He invents a comparative of a superlative noun to express himself more forcefully. Here was no mock modesty. There were times when he had to vindicate his apostleship, and on such occasions he could become, as he puts it, 'a fool' in his boastful confidence (2 Cor. 11.18ff.). Nevertheless, he had no illusions about himself. True saints grow more humble as they increase in holiness. The nearer we are to God the less we shall think of ourselves. William Carey, the pioneer missionary, was invited by the Governor General of India to a dinner party. Members of the aristocracy present tended to regard missionaries with scorn. Carey overheard one army officer say loudly, 'I believe Carey was a shoemaker, was he not, before he took up the profession of a missionary?' Carey at once interposed, 'Oh no! I was only a cobbler—I could mend shoes and was not ashamed.'

Whereas Paul belittled himself he always had the highest estimate of the ministry to which God had called him. To have been put in trust with the gospel was, to him, an honour of inestimable magnitude. Paul saw himself as conveying a message which centred in the person of Christ. Salvation for him meant more than the fact of forgiveness of past sins—it related to present enjoyment of God's goodness and future glory yet to be revealed. The phrase 'the unsearchable riches of Christ' (8) is noteworthy.

41

Someone has commented: 'Had Paul lived, preached and written until this present day, he had not exhausted the subject, nor fully declared the unsearchable riches of Christ.' We could no doubt include among those riches His essential glory as Creator, His divine condescension, His perfect manhood, His vicarious suffering and death, His priestly intercession, His promised return and future reign. All this, and much more, was included in the full-orbed gospel the apostle Paul felt called to preach.

30: By Divine Appointment

1 Timothy 1.12–17; 2 Timothy 1.8–14

In the first of these passages the apostle Paul refers to his personal experience of the gospel, giving us an autobiographical pen picture. The very thought of being entrusted with the gospel reminded Paul afresh of his own experience of God's saving grace. As one commentator has put it, 'If Christ can change Paul, the greatest of sinners, into an apostle, there is no limit to His transforming power. So, let no man say that his duties as a Christian are beyond his abilities' (Easton).

Paul never ceases to marvel that he, of all people, should have been called into the Lord's service. He certainly did not see himself as being self-appointed, but, rather, as divinely commissioned. He knew himself to be an outstanding example of what divine grace can accomplish in a human life. The Greek word rendered 'pattern' or 'example' (16) was the word used to describe the lightning sketch of an artist. Reflecting thus on God's infinite mercy the apostle bursts forth into adoring praise of God Himself, who had saved and commissioned one who had formerly been a blasphemer and a persecutor, a ring-leader among the enemies of Christ.

In his second letter Paul again testifies to God's saving grace and keeping power. A key verse in the passage is v. 12. He commissions his spiritual son, Timothy, to guard the truth that has been entrusted to him, and at the same time warns him that Christian service may well mean suffering as, indeed, Paul himself had experienced.

Paul's personal affirmation of his faith in v. 12 is calculated to be an encouragement to Timothy. The literal rendering of the Greek here is 'my deposit'. It may be taken either as referring to what God entrusted to Paul, or what Paul entrusted to God. Dr.

Alexander Maclaren comments: 'The metaphor is a plain enough one. A man has some rich treasure. He is afraid of losing it, he is doubtful of his own power of keeping it! He looks about for some reliable person and trusted hands, and he deposits it there.' The 'day' to which Paul refers is, no doubt, the Judgement Day, the day of final account.

The apostle Paul was never happier than when he spoke of the wonder of God's saving and keeping power. He never ceased to marvel at the fact of God's grace towards him. He would have rejoiced to sing—

Jesu, what didst Thou find in me
That Thou hast dealt so lovingly?

For him each day was lived in the light of the coming day of reckoning. George Meredith speaks somewhere of what he calls 'the rapture of the forward view'.

Questions and themes for study and discussion on Studies 26-30

1. What principles are there in our Lord's commission to the apostles for their evangelistic work which still apply today?
2. Why is our Lord's threefold commission to Peter of particular significance?
3. What was Paul's twofold commission?

43

SIX

Spiritual Oversight and Material Concern

Introduction

While it may be difficult to establish a regular pattern of ministry throughout the New Testament there is no doubt as to the caring spirit that prevailed. Leaders in the local church were charged, not only to be concerned with the spiritual well-being of the members, but also with their material needs. Authentic Christianity is concerned for 'the whole man'.

31: The Appointment of the Seven

Acts 6.1–7

It is generally assumed that in this passage we have the origin of the office of deacon. The seven men referred to were set apart by the apostles with prayer and the laying on of hands, to assist primarily in the administrative affairs of the church, though it is clear that they also fulfilled spiritual functions. Their main task, however, was to exercise responsibility in the everyday activities of the church, while the apostles spent the majority of the time in prayer and teaching.

One has to admit that while tradition has it that the seven mentioned in Acts 6 were the original deacons, they are not designated as such in the book of Acts. Indeed it could be argued that Luke would seem to be describing a purely temporary measure to deal with a particular situation. Some have contended that the seven are in fact the forerunners not of the diaconate but of the presbyterate. A few years later we read of money collected for distribution to the poor saints in Jerusalem which was placed in the hands of men who are called elders or presbyters. Whether the seven were in fact the original deacons or not there are of course later references in the New Testament to the existence of deacons as such. It is clear, for example, that there were deacons in the church at Philippi (Phil. 1.1). In his letter to Timothy Paul sets out clearly the qualifications for those who would hold this office (1 Tim. 3.8–13).

All we can conclude with any certainty is that the deacons in the early Church represented in the first instance an auxiliary ministry, appointed at the request of the apostles to assist them. As the pattern of the Church's ministry developed somewhat they found their place in assisting the elders or bishops in the local church.

The qualifications called for in the seven are such as should mark any who hold office in the Christian Church. Of them we know virtually nothing except in the case of Philip and Stephen, both of whom did a great deal more than 'serve tables', as the next few chapters of Acts clearly show.

32: The Office of Elder

Acts 11.27–30; 14.21–23; 20.25–32

The origin of elders (or presbyters) is less clear than that of deacons. The first reference to elders is in connection with the church at Jerusalem (Acts 11.30). We neither know who they were nor how they were appointed. Some suggest they may have been the seven of Acts 6 under an official title. Others have conjectured that they were the relieving-officers for the Hebrews, just as the seven were for the Hellenists. All such speculations are incapable of proof. The only reasonable certainty is that the title was borrowed from the presbyterate of the Jewish synagogue.

There are, of course, frequent references in the Old Testament to the 'elders of the people' or the 'elders of Israel'. These men were largely responsible for the administration of Jewish communal life. They had responsibilities in both civil and ecclesiastical affairs. It was their responsibility to study the law, to expound it, and to deal with those who had broken it. Jewish elders are referred to twenty-three times in the Gospels, and eight times in the rest of the New Testament. The first Christians were almost entirely made up of Jewish men and women, and so it is a reasonable inference that they took over the office of elder from the synagogue and its administration with which they were familiar. The Greek, *presbuteros*, is the equivalent of the Hebrew *zaqen* which was the term used after the Exile for the members of the

Jewish Sanhedrin which met under the chairmanship of the Jewish high priest.

There is no reference to elders at Antioch (Acts 13.1), nor are they mentioned in the apostle's earlier letters. Paul and Barnabas, however, on their first missionary journey appointed elders in all the churches they founded (Acts 14.23). It is clear that the elders whom Paul addressed at Ephesus (Acts 20.17ff.), and those addressed in the first epistle of Peter and referred to in the epistle to Titus had a decisive place in the life of the church. They shared in the ministry of Christ towards the flock (1 Pet. 5.1–4; Acts 20.28). In the New Testament the terms *episcopos* (bishop or overseer) and *presbuteros* (presbyter or elder) appear to be interchangeable. Paul, for example, calls for the elders of the church at Ephesus (Acts 20.17), and then addresses them as bishops (*episcopoi*, 28), translated overseers in the RSV.

It is clear that the office of elder carried with it a measure of authority. An elder was responsible for leadership in the church (1 Pet. 5.1–5). At the same time he had to be careful not to lord it over the people (1 Pet. 5.3). Younger Christians were encouraged to respect the elders (1 Pet. 5.5). The duties of presbyters included teaching and preaching the Word of God (1 Tim. 5.17) and anointing the sick (Jas. 5.14). Theirs was the task of episcopal oversight of the flock of God (Acts 20.28).

33: Qualifications for Leadership

1 Timothy 3.1–13

Whereas the New Testament does not appear to give a blueprint concerning church government it does set out very clearly definite qualifications which are required in those who are to be leaders in the Christian church.

In this particular passage two offices are mentioned specifically —that of bishop or overseer, and that of deacon. In the New Testament there is no exact equivalent of the concept of a bishop as generally understood today. At least until the time of Ignatius (around A.D. 115) the word bishop was used of those who exercised oversight in the local congregation and *episkopos* would therefore perhaps be the equivalent today of minister, presiding leader, or vicar.

In examining the qualifications required in Christian leaders it

46

is necessary to bear in mind that many church members had been converted against a background of extremely low moral standards. It was, therefore, essential that Christian leaders should be men of unquestioned moral integrity, and of blameless reputation in the local community. Qualities of temperament also come into the picture. Canon Liddon pointed out that we have here a picture of 'a man of calm, unimpassioned mind, collected, unexcitable, well composed'. Christian leaders should be those who think before they speak, and should possess sound judgement. Another essential quality is willingness to show hospitality. In the early days of the Church it was virtually impossible for a believer to accept hospitality in a pagan home. Christians as they journeyed from place to place were entertained by their fellow believers, and, of all people, the bishop must have open house. The Christian leader should not be a contentious or quarrelsome person, rubbing people up the wrong way, nor should he be a lover of money. Someone who is blatantly acquisitive is not a suitable person for leadership in the Christian church.

The qualifications for the deacon are only slightly less exacting. Those who hold office must not be tale-bearers or given to gossip; as has been pointed out: 'it is all too easy, even for Christian leaders, to become men pleasers and to accommodate their opinions to the company in which they find themselves.' It is significant that the deacon like the bishop or elder must have strong spiritual convictions. He must also be someone who has proved himself before being called upon to accept office. It is also noteworthy that one of the essential qualifications is that the leader must have the right kind of wife. A wife may make her husband ineligible for leadership if she herself is not absolutely trustworthy. She must be a true helper.

34: The Right Type of Leaders
Titus 1.5–16

The theme here is spiritual leadership in the local church. Titus has been given the responsibility for finding the right sort of leaders for the church in Crete. As in other similar passages the terms bishop (overseer) and elder appear to be used interchangeably, whereas the word steward, i.e. one who acts on behalf of another, is used of every servant of God. It is clear from the requirements

47

set out here that Christian leadership should be entrusted to mature men of God; men of blameless character and sober judgement. They should have a well ordered family life, and be gifted with obvious spiritual grace and understanding. Furthermore, it is essential for spiritual leaders to have settled doctrinal convictions and be able to encourage and teach others.

Every church reflects the social and cultural background of its members, factors which sometimes create their own special problems. This was true of Crete whose population had the reputation of being 'liars, evil beasts, lazy gluttons' (12). Christian leaders have to understand local conditions and act accordingly. In Crete it would not always be possible to mete out 'kid glove treatment'; sometimes they would need to be rebuked sharply. The apostle goes on to point out that the all-important thing is to see that in the local church Christian profession and practice shall go hand in hand. Paul speaks in strong language of those who profess to know God, but deny Him by their deeds (16).

He uses a word that was applied to coins below standard weight—worthless. These interlopers profess to 'know God', but the way they behave shows them up in their true colours. Their stock-in-trade consists solely in their plausible language.

Against a background of moral pollution, it is essential that those chosen to hold office in the Christian Church shall be above reproach. The unfortunate reputation of the Cretans is regrettably matched by many in our modern society. The problem of false teaching infiltrating the Christian Church is not new. At Crete some of the Jewish church members were guilty of hair-splitting legalism. They probably regarded the fact that they were circumcised as a mark of superiority entitling them to be looked up to by others. Those who deceive the people of God, whoever they are, must be silenced and it is the task of church leaders to do this. When the church is threatened in this way the need for wise leadership is of paramount importance. Thus, Paul instructs Titus to see to it that well-qualified elders are appointed to every Christian community (5). Such men must themselves know where they stand and be ready to defend the faith in the face of all opposition.

35: Respect for Church Leaders

Hebrews 13.7–17

In this passage the writer speaks particularly of attitudes towards

Christian leaders. The reference to ruling is not in the sense of governing, but rather of teaching and guiding. The Hebrew Christians were to study carefully the lives of their leaders, especially those who had died for the faith, and were to emulate them. Whether in life or in death they had borne testimony to the unchanging Christ in whom they trusted. Just as He had met their need in the past, so He can meet present and future needs. Because Christ is changeless the truth about Him is also changeless (8), and unbiblical doctrines are to be avoided (9). These Hebrew Christians were particularly warned against the idea that one cannot become 'properly established' without partaking of special sacral or sacrificial food (Stibbs). The really important thing is to have a living, personal relationship with God, which alone can give a man peace in the midst of changing circumstances.

The Christian 'altar' is Christ's death on the Cross and, therefore, the ceremonial observances under the old covenant are no longer relevant. Those who cling to Judaism and continue in the ritual of former days are deluded and do not share the benefits of Christ's death. Loyalty to Christ, however, may involve loss of friends, and the experience of reproach. Christians have to take their place with a Christ who has been rejected (outside the camp).

In the opening of this passage the Hebrew Christians were being exhorted to remember their spiritual leaders who had passed on. Now, in v. 17 the call is to obey those spiritual leaders still in their midst. It is not enough that we esteem our past leaders, our responsibility is to submit to present spiritual guides. Christian leaders carry a weighty responsibility and are accountable for the spiritual well-being of those placed in their care. Believers are to make the work of pastors and teachers lighter rather than heavier.

36: An Exhortation to Elders

1 Peter 5.1–5

In this paragraph Peter delineates the responsibilities of elders in the local church. Primarily they are responsible for pastoral care, supervising and instructing the people of God. This they are to do under the direction of 'the chief Shepherd' Himself (4).

It is important that they should do this in the right spirit, not because they must, but because they freely choose to do so. Furthermore, their motives must be right. They are not to engage in Christian service with material gain in mind, but to serve the Lord for the sheer joy of doing so. It is equally important that their attitude should be right—they are to lead the flock, rather than drive it; to give an example rather than domineer. They must always recognize that they are ultimately answerable to the chief Shepherd, who will reward them appropriately in the last great day. One rendering of v. 5 says, 'gird on humility as an apron'. It is significant that throughout the New Testament so much emphasis is placed upon the need for humility of mind and especially on the part of those, who, because of their office, might well be tempted to show an attitude of self-assertiveness. In his lectures to students preparing for the pastoral ministry Dr. Ernest Kevan used to say, 'beware of almightiness'.

It has already been suggested that in the early Church the terms bishop, pastor and elder were used interchangeably to describe those entrusted with pastoral oversight in the local church. In this connection it is significant that the apostle Peter, far from arrogating to himself exclusive privileges and powers, is happy to associate himself with the elders as their fellow elder when he has occasion to exhort them. Then, as if to break down the mere official distinction, he goes on to exhort the younger to be subject unto the elder, and all—old and young, rich and poor, official and private—all are encouraged to 'clothe themselves with humility toward one another' (5). There is no intention in the New Testament of turning the ministry of the gospel into a clerical caste by conferring exclusive rights and privileges, indeed there are frequent warnings against the temptation to fall into any such error. The whole drift of our Lord's teaching lies in an entirely different direction.

Questions and themes for study and discussion on Studies 31-36

1. What abiding lessons are there to be learned from the way the apostles handled the situation described in Acts 6.1-7?
2. What are the most essential qualities required in a Christian leader?
3. Outline some of the main differences between ministry under the Old Covenant and under the New.

SEVEN

Baptism

Introduction

Anyone reading the New Testament can hardly fail to see that baptism is a 'gospel sacrament'. The divine commission includes the command to baptize in the name of the triune God. The use of water as a symbol of cleansing is also beyond dispute, and generally accepted. The Christian Church is, however, sadly divided as to the subjects for and mode of baptism. The points at issue are whether the children of Christian parents are eligible for baptism, or it is to be regarded as an ordinance for believers only, and whether, in order to preserve the symbolism of the New Testament, total immersion is necessary. Over such issues there must be respect for diverse opinions, but whatever position we adopt, our understanding of the significance and importance of baptism will have much in common.

37: The Baptism of Our Lord

Luke 3.1–22

Here we are brought face to face with the preaching of John the Baptist whose ministry prepared the way for the Lord. John probably was preaching in the year A.D. 27 while the public ministry of Jesus commenced some six months later. At the time, both moral degeneration and political upheaval threatened the Roman Empire.

John the Baptist was a man of the desert and the crowds flocked out to hear him. The very way he lived convinced men he was a true prophet. Human applause and approbation meant nothing to him—he was utterly fearless in his preaching. He went right to the heart of things and presented religion in an entirely new light. He called upon his hearers to repent of their sins and to be baptized as an outward and visible sign of the genuineness of their repentance.

The truly surprising thing was that Jesus should come to

51

John for baptism. Understandably John was taken aback by this approach; the incongruity of it overwhelmed him. Here was the sinless Jesus seeking to undergo a baptism meant for sinners. Why, in fact, did our Lord take this step? The time for Him to begin His public ministry had arrived, and by being baptized He was showing His solidarity with fallen humanity. All through His earthly ministry He showed Himself a friend of tax collectors and sinners, and even at His death 'he was numbered with the transgressors' (Luke 22.37). Here, at the outset, He also took His stand by the side of sinners. It was the beginning of the work that was to be completed at Calvary when He was made sin on our behalf (2 Cor. 5.21).

At His baptism Jesus heard a voice and saw a vision. The voice was the call for which He had been waiting—the call to commence His ministry, while the vision was of a dove—the symbol of the Holy Spirit descending upon Him and endowing Him for Messiahship.

In New Testament times it was customary for Jewish proselytes to be baptized when they forsook heathendom and allied themselves with the people of God. There was something quite distinctive, however, about John's baptism. It was no mere ceremonial purification, but signified 'repentance for the remission of sins'. Furthermore, it was for Jews and not merely proselytes, and, most important of all, it was closely linked with preparation to meet the coming Messiah.

It is significant that, according to John's teaching, neither the observance of religious rites, nor a godly ancestry, are of any avail in providing for the sinner a way of escape from the divine judgement. None can opt out of the need of repentance. The two operative words for the seeking sinner are 'repent' and 'believe'.

38: Behold the Lamb!

John 1.19–34

The main theme of this passage is the witness of John the Baptist to Christ. The priests and Levites who came to John represented the religious life of the community. John was emphatic in pointing out he was not the Christ. Even the baptism that he gave was not comparable with His baptism. John's ministry consisted in preaching repentance and in pointing to the Christ, who was so much greater than he.

It is clear that the Jewish leaders regarded John as a very important person. He might have been the Messiah himself, or the prophet Elijah who was expected to appear, or 'the Prophet' whom some equated with Jeremiah. John was emphatic with his disclaimers—he was himself, and his mission was to bear witness to the Messiah. At the same time, he did not decry the importance of his own ministry. He was the Messiah's herald, and as such should be heeded. He was, in fact, the last of the Old Testament prophets, and in the assessment of Christ Himself, 'the greatest born of woman'. Whereas we must not over-rate ourselves, there is no value in self-depreciation. Each of us has a place to fill and John recognized his. He was concerned to point men to Jesus, whom he described as 'the Lamb of God'. This phrase conveys the thought of sacrifice, and John in using it anticipates Christ's atoning death on the Cross.

It seems from this passage that John had already baptized Jesus, and he had been led by prophetic insight to recognize Him as the Messiah—the One who would baptize with the Holy Spirit in due time. When John saw Jesus approaching him He recognized Him immediately. Though cousins they had probably not met until recently. John had spent his life in the seclusion of the desert, whereas Jesus had been in Galilee. It could well be that the two had not met until Jesus came to Jordan to be baptized by John. John expected that there would be some indication whereby he would recognize the Messiah, and as Jesus emerged from the Jordan the long-expected sign was given—the Spirit descended on Him from heaven like a dove. John the Baptist stands for all time as a shining example of what every Christian's witness should be. He was ready to stand aside and point to Christ rather than seek glory for himself.

39: The Forerunner
John 3.1–8; 3.22–4.3

Nicodemus was a scrupulous observer of the law, a Pharisee held in the highest esteem, and a ruler of the Jews. Nevertheless, he was fairly open-minded in certain respects. He had been intrigued by what he had heard about the teaching and miracles of Jesus of Nazareth and was eager to investigate for himself. He was even willing to admit that only a truly godly man could act in this way.

Our Lord met Nicodemus with a challenge—in spite of his

53

religious upbringing and position of leadership, he needed to be born anew. He could see beneath the surface and could discern Nicodemus' deep spiritual need, for all his outward religious profession. In effect Jesus was saying: 'God's mysteries are not the heritage of the learned, the moral, or the religious, simply because of learning, morality or religion; they are the heritage of the spiritually transformed' (Tenney).

Nicodemus was obviously nonplussed at this reference to new birth. He could think of birth along physical lines (4), but that could not be what Christ meant. At the same time how could a man at his time of life start all over again? Our Lord's words in reply to Nicodemus' query have been the subject of much discussion, particularly his reference to water. Was our Lord referring here to baptism? There are other New Testament references where water and Spirit are mentioned together in relation to baptism (cf. John 1.33; Matt. 3.11). Christ's teaching makes it clear that water baptism of itself is not sufficient. The sign needs to be accompanied by the thing signified—namely, the cleansing work of the Holy Spirit.

Following the interview Jesus and His disciples resorted to the country district of Judea and baptized, although our Lord did not Himself baptize (4.2). Meanwhile, further north, John was continuing to baptize those who came to him in repentance. Clearly, even at this early stage in His work, Jesus felt that baptism was of great importance. In common with John's baptism it would have been a sign of repentance but would have had the added dimension that here was One who was to baptize not only with water, but with the Spirit (cf. Mark 1.8). Although the full significance of Christian baptism could not emerge until after Christ's death, resurrection and ascension, and the coming of the Spirit at Pentecost, the baptism which Jesus and His disciples practised should be regarded 'as a guarantee of greater blessing to come' (Tasker). Already, however, baptism is taking on the character of an outward sign of an inward change ('being born of water and the Spirit', v. 5) and a public confession of the participant's identification with Christ and His Kingdom.

40: Misdirected Ambition
Mark 10.35–45; Luke 12.49–53

In this passage we have highlighted the unfortunate ambition of two of our Lord's disciples, James and John. Although they had lived so close to Him they had obviously failed to take heed both of His teaching and example. While He is about to lay down His very life, they are concerned with self-interest—seeking to ensure a place of prominence in the coming Kingdom. Jesus has to tell them sadly that they do not realize what they are asking. They have failed to realize that leadership in His Kingdom only comes to those who are prepared to suffer.

The word 'baptism' is used here by our Lord in a metaphorical sense. The cup stands for suffering and the baptism for overwhelming sorrow. Baptism is used in the Old Testament as a picture of one undergoing the wrath of God (Psa. 69.15). Christian baptism is 'into Christ's death' (Rom. 6.3), and is a reminder of the costliness of discipleship. Every disciple must, in some measure, drink from Christ's cup of sorrow and share in His baptism of suffering, and this very fact cuts right across the spirit which James and John were displaying in their attempt to secure personal glory.

Our Lord never left His followers in any doubt as to what it might mean to serve Him. He had not come to bring peace but a sword, and even within the confines of a family there might be friction and strife. Once more He uses the metaphor of baptism. He has 'an overwhelming baptism to come' (Berkeley). Baptism here must refer to the coming passion (cf. Mark 10.38f.). It has been said that the thought of Calvary was already a Gethsemane to the Lord. It is impossible to exaggerate the suspense and agony of anticipation (12.50).

Those of us who live in countries where we are spared from physical persecution for the sake of Christ need to remember our brothers who suffer for His sake. Even so, some of us may know in our own experience how becoming a Christian has caused a division in the family. We should not be surprised at this for we have been repeatedly warned that Christ came not 'to give peace on earth, but rather division'. Countless numbers of Christians across the world have experienced what it is to be baptized with this baptism.

41: Baptism in the Early Church

Acts 2.37–42; 8.9–13, 35–38

Peter's preaching on the Day of Pentecost brought about deep conviction in the hearts of his hearers. To those who truly repented Peter addressed a call to be baptized as a sign of their repentance and as a confession of their new-found faith in Jesus as Messiah. With this double demand for repentance and baptism he held out a double offer—the remission of their sins and the gift of the Holy Spirit. Baptism was to be in the name of Jesus—a clear indication that it signified an identification with Him, in His suffering and resurrection, in His present life and in the ethical and practical demands of His gospel. Four characteristics marked the life of these new converts—they showed a deep and continuing interest in the apostles' teaching; they entered into fellowship with one another; they obeyed Christ's injunction to remember Him in breaking of bread, and attended public prayer (42).

In the second passage we are introduced to the situation before Philip began his work in Samaria. Simon Magus was a magician who indulged in a good deal of self-advertisement and also in sorcery. He had remarkable success but his aims and motives were for his own glory rather than the glory of God. When Philip arrived on the scene, Simon believed and was baptized. We are bound to ask whether his motives were mixed, for he shows a certain amount of self-interest and later has an unhealthy concern for the more spectacular demonstrations of the Spirit's presence and the power which they would bring him. His belief that he could purchase the Spirit demonstrates a lack of understanding.

It was clearly possible in the Early Church for people to be baptized from wrong motives or without an adequate appreciation of the significance of the action. Baptism should never be undertaken lightly by those who make a profession of faith. It is a solemn, and in some senses irrevocable, step; a public and personal declaration of our faith in Christ, love for Him and determination to follow Him whatever the cost, a symbolic act which should be a means of cementing our relationship with Him and drawing strength from Him.

In the story of the baptism of the Ethiopian eunuch we have an example of the stages which would normally precede baptism. The eunuch was an honest seeker after truth—he was searching the Scriptures and through the illumination of the Holy Spirit he was brought face to face with Jesus Christ. It is clear that he must have repented of his sin there and then and turned to Christ as Saviour. With the minimum of delay he sought baptism. At the time of his baptism the eunuch could have known little theology, but he had a clear grasp of his own condition and of what Christ had done for him. He had believed and that fact was enough to warrant Philip baptizing him. No doubt Philip had told him about baptism as being the way by which new converts may confess their faith in Christ, and express their identity with Him. That being so, the eunuch's desire is natural and Philip's willingness to baptize him shows the importance attached to baptism by the Early Church as a sign of entry into the Kingdom.

42: Converts Baptized
Acts 16.11–15, 25–34

Ramsay comments, 'It is remarkable with what interest Luke records the incidents from harbour to harbour. He has the true Greek feeling for the sea.' Neapolis was the harbour of Philippi. The Roman colonies were primarily intended as military safeguards and were, in fact, representations in miniature of the Roman people. Philippi contained no synagogue and practically no Jews. It was a military rather than a commercial centre. Those who were Jews or Jewish proselytes were accustomed to gather for prayer by a riverside. Among the company on this occasion was Lydia, a native of Thyatira, which was famous for its dyeing. The fact that she traded in purple-dyed garments suggests that she was a woman of position and means. She was herself a Jewish proselyte, and seems to have had an influence over her whole household. It is interesting to note the different ways in which men and women are converted in Acts. In the case of the Philippian jailer there was an element of fear, in the case of Saul conversion was a most dramatic experience, whereas Lydia simply 'opened her heart'.

In common with the other converts of whom we read in Acts, Lydia lost no time in seeking baptism. Furthermore, members of her household were baptized with her. It has, of course, long been a point of discussion as to whether there were any children involved.

It is remarkable that Paul and Silas were able to sing when they had been so cruelly wronged and were cooped up in a stifling cell in the utmost discomfort. Their wounds had not been treated and they had been left without food. When the earthquake struck, the prisoners were terrified, and seemed to make no attempt to escape. Paul and Silas alone remained self-possessed. The jailer was filled with fear, and on the point of suicide until restrained by Paul. He asks the momentous question, 'What must I do to be saved?'

And the answer he immediately received was simple and authoritative—salvation demands faith in a person, and even faith itself is a free gift of God's grace. As in the case of Lydia, so here the household is included. The reality of the jailer's conversion was expressed in a most practical way for he immediately washed the wounds of his prisoners, and he too was baptized 'with all his family' without delay. Here again, it must remain an open question as to whether all who were baptized with him consciously heard, understood and personally responded to the preaching of the gospel.

43: Baptism in the Name of the Lord Jesus

Acts 19.1-7

Paul, having visited the churches of south Galatia now pays a return visit to Ephesus. He soon came across a number of professing disciples who appeared to be entirely ignorant of the existence of the Holy Spirit. Some have suggested they may not have been Christians at all, but this would seem unlikely in view of the fact that they are called disciples. Furthermore, Paul asked them if they received the Holy Spirit when they believed, indicating that he took them to be true believers. It could be, of course, that the apostle was mistaken. They had, in fact, been disciples of John the Baptist, and it is hard to think that they had no knowledge whatever of the Holy Spirit, but certainly they were not conscious of His active presence. They had been baptized by John the Baptist and it is important to remember that his was a baptism of expectation rather than fulfilment. Now they are baptized into the name of the Lord Jesus, and when Paul laid his hands on them they received the gift of the Holy Spirit with outward manifestations. These twelve disciples perhaps became the nucleus of the Ephesian church.

Receiving the Holy Spirit is a subject which causes a great deal of discussion. It is clear from the Acts that every believer shares in the gift of the Spirit. The confession of Jesus as Lord is the unfailing sign of the Spirit's presence (1 Cor. 12.3). There are, in fact, four outstanding instances in the Acts of believers 'receiving the Holy Spirit' (2.1-4; 8.14 ff; 10.44-48; 19.1-7). In each case a number of believers were involved, and in most cases certain unusual manifestations followed. We suggest that in these instances it was clearly necessary that there should be an immediate proof that He had, in fact, been received. The time and manner of the Spirit's coming differed, however, in each case. In one case the Spirit came before baptism, in two cases after baptism, and in two cases through the laying on of hands of an apostle. Paul makes it clear 'Anyone who does not have the Spirit of Christ does not belong to him' (Rom. 8.9). Every true believer is indwelt by the Holy Spirit, but we are told to be filled with the Spirit (Eph. 5.18). Incidentally, this incident in Acts ch. 19 is the last occasion on which we read of the Holy Spirit being given and of those receiving Him speaking with tongues.

44: Baptism into Christ

Romans 6

In the early chapters of Romans Paul has been primarily concerned with the subject of justification by faith—how the sinful are accounted righteous because of Christ's atoning sacrifice solely on the basis of saving faith. He now turns to the subject of holy living, dealing with those who might be tempted to argue, 'If God's grace abounds and triumphs so wonderfully, let us go on sinning so as to bring out that grace more and more.' In refuting any such notion the apostle points out that pardon is to be seen as the cause and producer of holiness. In pursuing this argument Paul introduces the subject of baptism.

He speaks of believers as being baptized into Christ (cf. Gal. 3.27). Baptism is seen as a symbol of our death and burial with Christ. A. B. Simpson comments: 'There must be an actual yielding of the life to be crucified with Christ. There is a moment when we consent to die. . . . It is assumed by the apostle that we did this in our baptism.' While the rite of baptism pictures our death and burial it does not bring it about. We may be partakers of the outward seal and yet lack the inward reality.

But Christ did not remain buried, He rose to a new life; so it should be with His people. Those who see themselves as having died with Christ, by faith, identify themselves also with His resurrection. The same supernatural power which raised Christ from the dead is available to Christians to enable them to walk in newness of life (4). A Christian shares the death of Christ—but more than that, he also shares His resurrection.

Those Christians who feel that the only valid form of baptism is by immersion base their arguments very largely on this passage. They point out that only when the candidate is totally immersed does he really enact what it means to be buried with Christ. If, as many would feel, the passage refers to water baptism, it is clear that the apostle assumed that every professing Christian would have been baptized. Baptism is seen to signify union with Christ. The phrase frequently used in the New Testament is 'baptized into Christ', or 'into the name of Christ' (Acts 8.16; 19.5; Gal. 3.27). Union with Christ, invisibly effected by faith, is visibly signified and sealed by baptism. Just as being immersed represents burial with Christ, so coming up out of the waters of baptism represents the believer entering into newness of life. Thus a Christian, by faith inwardly and by baptism outwardly, has been united to Christ in His death and resurrection.

Questions and themes for study and discussion on Studies 37-45

1. What was the special significance of John's baptism (Luke 3)?
2. What was the relationship between conversion and baptism in the early Church?
3. What were the particular differences between John's baptism and Christian baptism as seen in Acts 19.1–7?
4. In what sense may we regard baptism as a visual aid (Rom. 6)?

EIGHT

The Lord's Supper

Introduction

It is one of the greatest tragedies of the Christian Church that the Lord's Supper, which should be a focal point of the unity of believers, has become the occasion of such disunity. There are Christians who will work and witness with other Christians yet feel unable to join them at the Lord's table.

In the New Testament we find a number of different phrases used to describe this commemorative feast. It is the Lord's Supper (1 Cor. 11.20), the Lord's Table (1 Cor. 10.21), the Breaking of bread (Acts 2.42; 20.7). Some Christians refer to it as a Eucharist (Thanksgiving), while the term Holy Communion derived, no doubt, from 1 Cor. 10.16 is probably the most commonly used expression of all.

45: The Last Supper

Luke 22.1–23

The chapter opens with the account of the treason of Judas. The Day of Unleavened Bread on which the Passover lamb had to be sacrificed, the fourteenth Nisan, saw Peter and John going to prepare for the meal. The householder, no doubt a friend of the Lord's, had a large upper room suitably furnished with cushions spread on the benches. At the appropriate hour just after sunset, Jesus and the disciples reclined on the benches to eat the Passover meal. In the account of this the cup is mentioned first, before the bread. At the Passover four or even five cups were passed round, and all would partake. It is noteworthy that before our Lord passed it to His disciples He paused to give thanks, and in any service of Holy Communion thanksgiving should always play a prominent part. As for our Lord Himself, He makes it clear that He will join in no more festivals till He rejoices in the completed Kingdom. The bread which He took would have been a flat cake of unleavened bread. Verse 20 does

61

not appear in all of the ancient manuscripts, but in the inauguration of the Lord's Supper the bread and the cup are always associated together.

Our Lord introduced the notion of a new covenant or agreement between God and man, of which His blood is the sign and seal. This word covenant calls attention to the federal aspect of the Lord's Supper. Covenants in the Old Testament were associated with covenant signs or seals, and so it is here. They witness to God's promise and pledge, and also to our attitude of acceptance.

When Christ said 'This is my body', He conveyed the idea that in the bread was an emblem of His body, and, similarly, the cup represents the new covenant which is to be sealed and ratified with His blood. Our Lord was speaking to Jews and it would have been unthinkable for them to drink literal blood (Lev. 3.17; 7.26).

It does seem as though Judas Iscariot was one of those who received the Lord's Supper, yet he was a 'son of perdition'. We all need to heed the warning to examine ourselves before we take part in such a service (1 Cor. 11.28–30).

46: A Word of Warning

1 Corinthians 10.14–22

Some Corinthian Christians had been accepting invitations to dine in the homes of their pagan neighbours. Not infrequently they would be presented with food which previously had been offered in sacrifice in a heathen temple. Paul has no objection to their accepting this hospitality, although he does warn that they should be careful to consider all the issues involved (27–30). When, however, it was a question of taking part in a meal explicitly linked with pagan worship (perhaps demanded by their membership of a trade-guild or other official body) it was a different matter. Heathen worshippers would feel that in eating meat or drinking wine which had formed part of a sacrifice they were in some sense identifying themselves with the deity. It was much the same in ancient Israel. In the Jewish ritual, the worshippers who ate the remainder of a sacrifice became 'partners in the altar' (18). The underlying idea here is that to feast on food offered in sacrifice is to have a ceremonial link with the deity at whose altar the food has been presented. Paul is calling upon

Christians to dissociate themselves completely from idol feasts. There can be no compromise in this respect.

The 'bread' and the 'cup' are regarded as things parallel to the food and wine of a pagan sacrifice meal. As was the sacred meal to the Israelite or the idol feast to the heathen worshipper in contemporary Corinth, so is the Supper of the Lord to the Christian.

The 'cup of blessing' was the name given to the third cup in the Passover feast and it may be assumed that this was the cup used by our Lord in instituting the Last Supper. A prayer of thanksgiving would be offered over the cup. A single loaf of bread would have been used and this in itself symbolized the unity of believers in Christ.

The main point the apostle is bringing out here is that feeding at the table of the Lord means having fellowship with Him as well as with His people, whereas participation in an idol feast means having fellowship with demons, and the two are incompatible. It is not enough to regard idols as being of no significance—heathen worship is offered to superhuman powers and seeks to establish communion with them and must, therefore, be taken seriously. God is a jealous God and seeks the entire devotion of His people.

47: The Need for Self-examination

1 Corinthians 11.17–34

This is probably the earliest account we have of the institution of the Lord's Supper. The apostle is concerned to correct certain abuses which had crept into the local observance of the Supper. Instead of being a blessing to the church, the service was having a disruptive effect. A party spirit had crept in and the essential purpose of the Lord's Supper was being overlooked. Differences between rich and poor were being accentuated. The common meal was a travesty of an *agape*, a love-feast. Each ate the food he had brought with him and the rich and the poor did not share their meal. Some were even drunk.

We cannot be sure just what the apostle means when he says he received from the Lord the command relating to the institution of the Lord's Supper. It could mean he had a special revelation, but may refer to the fact that he was passing on teaching that emanated from the Lord, having been transmitted through others

63

to him. Paul stresses the poignancy of the fact that the institution of the Supper took place on the very night when the Lord was being betrayed. A number of other interesting points emerge from this passage—the Supper is a means of actual proclamation of the Lord's death; there is grave danger in participating in the Supper without due consideration for its sacred and solemn meaning; there is a close connection between the Supper and the Second Advent.

The point that the apostle emphasizes is that coming to the Lord's Table calls for self-examination (28–29). The word here is also used in connection with the testing of metals. We should not lightly take part in a service of holy communion. Paul is not saying that to participate unworthily will incur eternal damnation, but he is saying that to do so is to bring upon oneself very real punishment, as the Corinthians themselves had done (30). 'Not to discern the body' means to fail to pay due regard to the solemnity of the occasion.

Verses 30–32 have occasioned a great deal of comment. Paul appears to be saying that the reason why some Christians have died and others suffer ill-health is due to a wrong attitude towards this service. Such divine judgement is of the Lord's goodness since otherwise those concerned might find themselves bracketed with the heathen world and sharing in its condemnation. However difficult these verses may be for us to understand, the overall demand for a serious approach comes to us as clearly as to the Corinthians. The two things that matter more than anything else as we come to the Table are that we should be in a right relationship with the Lord and with our fellow believers.

Questions and themes for study and discussion on Studies 45–47

1. Trace the connection between the Jewish Passover and the Christian service of Holy Communion.
2. What is to be understood from the metaphors of eating and drinking regarding our relationship to Christ? (John 6).
3. What abiding lessons are there from Paul's teaching regarding eating meat offered to idols? (1 Cor. 10).
4. What is the chief significance of the Lord's Supper? (1 Cor. 11. 23–26).